NEIL T. ANDERSON

THE
BONDAGE
BREAKER

MONARCH
Crowborough

First published in the USA by
Harvest House Publishers, Eugene, Oregon 97402

First British edition 1993
Reprinted 1993
Reprinted 1994, 1995

ISBN 1 85424 184 2

Some of the names in this book have been changed to protect the
privacy of the individuals involved.

Unless otherwise indicated, Scripture quotations in this publication are from the
NASB — New American Standard Bible. © 1960, 1962, 1963, 1968, 1971, 1972, 1973,
1975, 1977 by The Lockman Foundation.
Used by permission.

Other versions used are: *KJV — King James Version.*
NIV — Scripture quotations marked (NIV) are from the *Holy Bible, New
International Version.* Copyright © 1973, 1978, 1984, International Bible Society.
Used by permission of Zondervan Bible Publishers.

British Library Cataloguing in Publication Data
A catalogue record for this book is available from the British Library.

Designed and Produced in England for
MONARCH PUBLICATIONS
The Broadway, Crowborough, East Sussex, Kent TN6 1HQ
by Nuprint Ltd, Station Road, Harpenden, Herts AL5 4SE.

CONTENTS

ACKNOWLEDGMENTS

Four years ago at a Biola University faculty retreat, I asked my colleagues to pray about this book. I knew I needed to say something, but I really didn't want to. I wasn't afraid of spiritual opposition; I just didn't want the hassle which this topic inevitably stirs up in the Christian academic community. I wish I could say that all of us who teach at the graduate level are open-minded toward new ideas and differing worldviews, but it seems that the more educated we become, the more we defend our own perspectives. With an undergraduate degree in electronic engineering, two master's degrees, and two doctorates, I certainly qualify for this possibility.

That's why I'm so grateful to my students at Talbot School of Theology who constantly challenge me to stay true to my deepest commitment: biblical truth. No person helps me more in this area than my dear colleague Dr. Robert Saucy. I am fully aware of my need to be accountable to others, not just for moral reasons, but for credibility and integrity. Bob, you have been my rudder (and sometimes my anchor when I was tempted to proceed without due reflection) in the sea of spiritual conflicts. I'm indebted to you.

This book was not written by an academician who lacks experience on the battlefield. I have stood in the trenches for years, helping the victims of unspeakable abuse find release from the enemy of our souls. If I had known the price my family would pay for the path I have taken, I wouldn't have come this way. Part of that price has resulted from the conviction that I cannot charge others for a ministry of grace. I remember my young son asking, "Dad, would we have been better off if you had stayed an engineer?" In some ways, perhaps so. But, looking back, I can truly say I'm glad I came this way. Joanne, Heidi, and Karl, I love you dearly, and I and many others thank you for bearing a load you never asked for.

I want to acknowledge all of you good people who poured out your lives to me as we walked together into your freedom in Christ. There were many emotional moments remembering the pain and torment you suffered. I have learned from each of you as you shared your spiritual journeys with me. What a privilege for me to see God demonstrate His sufficient grace in your lives!

I want to thank Carolina and Mike Cranford for inputting the original content of the manuscript, and Ed Stewart for transforming the content into publishable form. Eileen Mason and the crew at Harvest House have been tremendously supportive. You people made this book possible.

I deeply appreciate those of you who contributed financially to make possible the videotaping of my conference. But no one has been more helpful to this ministry than Jerry and Sally Friesen. You are my partners, and I dedicate this book to you. Thank you for believing in me and committing yourself so faithfully to me and the ongoing ministry of Christ. I love you both.

—Neil T. Anderson

Free at Last!

A few years ago I was speaking in a Southern California church on the subject of the New Age movement. My text was 1 Timothy 4:1: "The Spirit explicitly says that in later times some will fall away from the faith, paying attention to deceitful spirits and doctrines of demons." After my message I was surrounded at the front of the sanctuary by people wanting to hear more about freedom from spiritual conflicts caused by demonic influences.

Sitting about halfway back in the sanctuary was a 22-year-old woman who had been weeping uncontrollably since the service ended. Several people had tried to comfort her, but she wouldn't allow anyone to get near her. Finally a church staff member cut through the crowd around me and said, "I'm sorry, folks, but we need Dr. Anderson back here right away."

As I approached the young woman I could hear her sobbing, "He understands! He understands!" We were able to get her out of the sanctuary and into a private office. After she calmed down, I scheduled an appointment with her for the next week.

When Nancy arrived for her appointment her face was marked by ugly, open scratch wounds. "I've been scratching myself like this, and I can't control it," she admitted sheepishly.

Nancy described her horrible childhood, which included an abusive father and a grandmother who identified herself as a black witch. "When I was three years old I received my guardians—spirit guides," she continued. "They were my companions, telling me how to live and what to say. I never questioned if having spirit guides was anything but normal until my mother took me to Sunday school. Then I began to suspect that my inner companions might not be good for me. When I asked my parents about it, my father beat me. I never asked again!"

In order to cope with the increasing torment that her spirit guides brought to her life, Nancy resorted to rigid personal discipline. In her high school years she trusted Christ as her Savior. But instead of leaving her, her "guardians" continued to harass her.

After high school Nancy turned to the epitome of discipline: the Marines. Determined to become the toughest of the lady leathernecks, she won awards for her discipline. But her spiritual torment kept pushing her mind and emotions to the edge. She refused to tell anyone about her mental battle for fear that she would be labeled insane. Finally the pressure overcame her and she snapped. Nancy quietly accepted a medical discharge and retreated to a lonely existence of inner turmoil and pain. This was Nancy's condition when she came to church and heard me talk about deceiving spirits.

"Finally someone understands me!" Nancy concluded tearfully.

"Would you like to get rid of your spirit guides?" I asked.

There was a long pause. "Will they really leave, or will I go home and be thrashed by them again?"

"You will be free," I assured her.

An hour later Nancy *was* free—and was hugging us with an openness she had never known before. "Now I can have people over to my house!" she exclaimed joyfully.

The Reality of the Dark Side

Nancy's experience is not an obscure, erratic blip in the contemporary Christian community. In fact, in more than 20 years of ministry as a pastor, counselor, seminary professor, and conference speaker, I have met and ministered to more Christians in bondage to the dark side of the spiritual world than you may believe.

My own journey into this realm of ministry did not come by choice. I was an aerospace engineer before God called me into ministry. Even as a Christian layman I was never curious about demon activity or the occult. The lure of esoteric knowledge and occultic power never appealed to me.

On the other hand, I have always been disposed to believe what the Bible says about the spiritual world even when it conflicts with accepted opinion. As a result, over 15 years ago the Lord began to direct me to Christians like Nancy who were in bondage to various forms of satanism and the occult. Also, I began to meet many believers who were controlled by thought patterns, habits, and behaviors which blocked their growth. My desire was to see these people free to live productive lives, but my training hadn't equipped me well in this area. I fumbled my way through a lot of failure in my early attempts to minister to them, but I also experienced some surprising success. I have concluded that Christians are woefully unprepared to deal with the dark world of Satan's kingdom or to minister to those who are in bondage to it

God Wants You Mature and Free

Through these years of learning and ministering I have come to understand that there are two concepts which determine the victory and fruitfulness of a Christian. The first concept is *maturity*. Paul wrote: "We are to grow up in all aspects into Him, who is the head, even Christ . . . to a mature man, to the measure of the stature which belongs to the fulness of Christ" (Ephesians 4:15,13). God has given us everything we need to grow to maturity in Christ (2 Peter 1:3). But Satan is opposed to our maturity and will do anything he can to keep us from realizing who we are and what we have in Christ. Since we wrestle against principalities

11

and powers instead of flesh and blood (Ephesians 6:12), we must experience victory over the dark side before we can fully mature.

My book, *Victory Over the Darkness* (Regal Books), focuses on the believer's walk by faith and maturity in Christ and identifies Satan's strategies designed to obstruct them. The book deals with the foundational issues of your identity in Christ and outlines practical steps on how to live by faith, walk according to the Spirit, renew your mind, manage your emotions, and resolve the emotional traumas of your past through faith and forgiveness. I strongly suggest that you work through *Victory Over the Darkness* in conjunction with your study of this book.

The second concept of the successful Christian life is *freedom*, which is the central theme of *The Bondage Breaker*. Paul declared: "It was for freedom that Christ set us free; therefore keep standing firm and do not be subject again to a yoke of slavery" (Galatians 5:1). This verse not only assures us that God wants us free, but warns us that we can lose our freedom.

Before we received Christ, we were slaves to sin. But because of Christ's work on the cross, sin's power over us has been broken. Satan has no right of ownership or authority over us. He is a defeated foe, but he is committed to keeping us from realizing that. He knows he can block your effectiveness as a Christian if he can deceive you into believing that you are nothing but a product of your past, subject to sin, prone to failure, and controlled by your habits. As long as he can confuse you and blind you with his dark lies, you won't be able to see that the chains which once bound you are broken. You are free in Christ, but if the devil can deceive you into believing you're not, you won't experience the freedom which is your inheritance. I don't believe in instant maturity, but I do believe in instant freedom, and I have seen thousands of people set free by the truth. Once a person is free, you would be amazed at how quickly he or she matures!

In this book I have attempted to clarify the nature of spiritual conflicts and outline how they can be resolved in Christ. Part One explains your position of freedom, protection, and authority in Christ. Part Two warns of your vulnerability to very real and very personal demonic influences which are intent on robbing you of your freedom through temptation, accusation, deception, and control. Part Three presents the steps to freedom in Christ which will help you walk free of the enemy's designs on your life.

The contrast between bondage and freedom in a believer's life is beautifully illustrated in the following letter from a successful professional man. Unlike Nancy, to all appearances this man was a normal, churchgoing Christian who was successful in his family and career. But he wasn't free.

Dear Neil,

I contacted you because I had been experiencing a host of seemingly inexplicable "psychologically related" attacks. My emotional troubles were probably rooted in my childhood experiences with horror movies, Ouija boards, etc. I clearly remember fearing a visit from devilish forces after I saw the movie titled *The Blood of Dracula*.

My father had a pretty hot temper and was given to emotional outbursts. My survival response was to sulk and blame myself for upsetting him. Bottling my emotions inside became a way of life. As I grew into adulthood I continued to blame myself for any and all personal shortcomings and misfortunes.

Then I accepted Christ as my personal Lord and Savior. I grew spiritually over the next several years, but I never enjoyed complete peace. There was always a lingering doubt about my relationship with God, whom I saw as distant and stern. I had difficulty praying, reading the Bible, and paying attention to the pastor's sermons. I seriously questioned the purpose of life. I experienced horrible nightmares which woke me up screaming.

It was during my time of prayer with you that I finally found freedom in Christ. I realized that God is not a harsh, aloof disciplinarian, but a loving Father who takes joy in my accomplishments. I also experienced a great release when I prayed to cancel out all demonic working that has been passed on to me from my ancestors.

Now when I read God's Word I understand it like never before. I have developed a more positive attitude, and my entire relationship with my Lord has completely changed. Since our meeting I haven't had one nightmare.

Neil, I'm afraid there are many Christians like me out there leading lives of "quiet desperation" due to the attack of demonic forces. If I can fall prey to these forces and seem all right, so can others.

Sincerely,

Public School District
Superintendent

Are you one of those Christians who lives in the quiet desperation of bondage to fear, anger, depression, habits you can't break, thoughts or inner voices you can't elude, or sinful behavior you can't escape? I'm not saying that every spiritual problem is the result of direct demonic activity. But you may be in bondage because you have overlooked or denied the reality of demonic powers at work in the world today. Your inheritance in Christ is the complete freedom He promises in the Scriptures, as exemplified in the testimonies of Nancy, the superintendent, and many others that you will read about in the pages ahead. Let me introduce you to the one who has already overcome the darkness and secured your freedom: Jesus Christ the Bondage Breaker!

PART ONE

Take Courage!

1

You Don't Have to Live in the Shadows

In the early 1980's I counseled a Christian young woman who was languishing in deep spiritual, mental, and emotional turmoil. At one point before our series of sessions she wrote the following prayer to God, then ten minutes later tried unsuccessfully to kill herself with an overdose of pills:

> Dear God,
>
> Where are you? How can you watch and not help me? I hurt so bad, and you don't even care. If you cared you'd make it stop or let me die. I love you, but you seem so far away. I can't hear you or feel you or see you, but I'm supposed to believe you're here. Lord, I feel them and hear them. They are here. I know you're real, God, but they are more real to me right now. Please make someone believe me, Lord. Why won't you make it stop? Please, Lord, please! If you love me you'll let me die.
>
> —A Lost Sheep

Over the past 20 years I have encountered hundreds of Christians like the woman who wrote this heartrending note. Most of them didn't attempt suicide as this one did, but many of them talked about dark impressions to do so. And nearly all of them admitted to the presence of "them"— inner urges or voices which badgered them, tempted and taunted them, accused them, or threatened them. I often warn people who make appointments to talk with me that they will "hear" messages such as "Don't go; he can't help you," or they will think disruptive thoughts in first-person singular like "I don't want to go" or "I've tried this before and it didn't work." One person wrote: "Every time I try to talk to you, or even think about talking to you, I completely shut down. Voices inside literally yell at me: 'No!' I've even considered killing myself to end this terrible battle going on inside. I need help!"

Many other Christians I deal with don't complain about hearing voices as such, but their minds are filled with such confusion that their daily walk with Christ is unfulfilling and unproductive. When they try to pray they begin thinking about a million things they should be doing. When they sit down to read the Bible or a good Christian book they can't concentrate, or they read for several minutes and suddenly realize that their thoughts have been a million miles away. When they have an opportunity to serve the Lord in some way they are brought up short by discouraging thoughts of self-doubt: "I'm not a strong Christian"; "I don't know enough about the Bible"; "I'm still plagued by sinful thoughts"; or "I don't have many spiritual gifts." Instead of being victorious, productive, joy-filled Christians, they trudge through life under a cloud just trying to hang on until Jesus comes. Some of this is certainly our own lack of mental discipline, but it can also reflect deception from the enemy. I have seen hundreds of people freed from this kind of deception.

COMMON MISCONCEPTIONS ABOUT BONDAGE

Where do the voices and the confusion come from? Where do the divergent thoughts and the condemning emotions originate? One of the main reasons I fumbled and failed in my early days of ministering to people in bondage was because I didn't know the real answers to these questions. I labored under a number of misconceptions about the spiritual world which had to be dispelled. Perhaps you are struggling with some of these same faulty ideas which keep Christians in darkness.

1. *Demons were active when Christ was on earth, but their activity has subsided today.* Christians who hold this extreme view in light of what God's Word says and what is transpiring in the world today simply are not facing reality. The New Testament clearly states that believers will wrestle "against the rulers, against the powers, against the world forces of this darkness, against the spiritual forces of wickedness in the heavenly places" (Ephesians 6:12). Paul goes on to itemize the pieces of spiritual armor that we are to put on in order to defend ourselves against "the flaming missiles of the evil one" (verses 13-17). In 2 Corinthians 10:3-5 Paul again specifies that believers are engaged in a spiritual battle against forces which stand against the knowledge of God. If dark spiritual powers are no longer attacking believers, why would Paul alert us to them and insist that we arm ourselves against them?

The powers and forces that Paul wrote about in the first century are still evident at the dawn of the twenty-first century, as evident in the popularity of the New Age movement and the proliferation of satanism and the occult.

God's people wrestling against dark spiritual forces is not a first-century phenomenon, nor is it an option for the Christian today; it's unavoidable. The kingdom of darkness is still present, and Satan is intent on making your life miserable and keeping you from enjoying and exercising your inheritance in Christ. Your only options in the conflict are how and to what extent you're going to wage the battle. If your worldview as a Christian does not include the kingdom of darkness, then either God or you will have to take a bum rap for all the corruption Satan is foisting on you and the rest of the world.

2. *What the early church called demonic activity we now understand to be mental illness.* I heard one counselor argue

concerning a demonically disturbed Christian, "There is no way his problem can be demonic; he's a paranoid schizophrenic." Simply accepting secular psychology's definition of a human problem in no way establishes the actual cause of the problem. Terms such as schizophrenia, paranoia, psychosis, etc., are merely labels classifying symptoms. But what or who is causing the symptoms? Is it a neurological or hormonal problem, or perhaps a chemical imbalance? Certainly these options must be explored. But what if no physical cause is found? Then it must be a psychological problem. But which school of psychology do you choose: biblical or secular? And why isn't someone exploring the possibility that the problem is primarily spiritual?

We should not be surprised that secular psychologists limited to a natural worldview supply only natural explanations for mental problems. They offer their explanation from a viewpoint with no concept of God, much less the demonic. Even many Christians who vociferously reject the scientific community's explanation for the origin of the species naively accept the secular psychologist's explanation of mental illness. Research based on the scientific method of investigation of human spiritual problems is not wrong; it's just incomplete. It ignores the influence of the spiritual world because neither God nor the devil submit to our methods of investigation.

3. *Some problems are psychological and some are spiritual.* This misconception implies a division between the human soul and spirit, which does not exist. There is no inner conflict which is not psychological, because there is never a time when your mind, emotions, and will are not involved. Similarly, there is no problem which is not spiritual. There is no time when God is not present or when it is safe for you to take off the armor of God. The tendency is to polarize into a deliverance ministry, ignoring the realities of the physical realm, or a psychotherapeutic ministry, ignoring the spiritual realm.

Dr. Paul Hiebert, who teaches in the School of Missions at Fuller Theological Seminary, contends that, as long as believers accept "a two-tier worldview with God confined to the supernatural and the natural world operating for all practical purposes according to autonomous scientific laws, Christianity will continue to be a secularizing force in the world."[1] If your worldview does not recognize the activity of the god of this world in human problems, it is at best incomplete and at worst a distortion of reality.

4. *Christians aren't subject to demon activity.* The prevailing belief among evangelicals today is that Christians cannot be severely oppressed by demons. Even the suggestion that demonic influence can be part of the problem often prompts the hasty disclaimer, "Impossible! I'm a Christian!"

Nothing has done greater damage to diagnosing spiritual problems than this untruth. If Satan can't touch the church, why are we instructed to put on the armor of God, to resist the devil, to stand firm, and to be alert? If we aren't susceptible to being wounded or trapped by Satan, why does Paul describe our relationship to the powers of darkness as a wrestling match? Those who deny the enemy's potential for destruction are the most vulnerable to it. Our vulnerability to demonic intrusion and influence is the subject of Part Two of this book.

5. *Demonic influence is only evident in extreme or violent behavior and gross sin.* Although there are cases today like the wild demoniac called "Legion" in Luke 8, most Christians suffering from demonic activity lead relatively normal lives while experiencing serious personal and interpersonal problems for which no cause or solution has been found. Since they relegate satanic involvement only to mass murderers or violent sex criminals, these ordinary problem-plagued individuals wonder what's wrong with them and why they can't just "do better."

Satan's first and foremost strategy is deception. Paul warned: "Satan disguises himself as an angel of light.

Therefore it is not surprising if his servants also disguise themselves as servants of righteousness" (2 Corinthians 11:14,15). It is not the few raving demoniacs which are causing the church to be ineffective, but Satan's subtle deception and intrusion into the lives of "normal" believers. One Christian psychotherapist who attended my conference on spiritual conflicts and counseling said, "I had never seen any evidence of demonism in all my years of counseling until I came to your conference. When I returned to my practice I discovered that two-thirds of my clients were having problems because they were being deceived by Satan—and so was I!"

6. *Freedom from spiritual bondage is the result of a power encounter with demonic forces.* Freedom from spiritual conflicts and bondage is not a power encounter; it's a truth encounter. Satan is a deceiver, and he will work undercover at all costs. But the truth of God's Word exposes him and his lie. His demons are like cockroaches that scurry for the shadows when the light comes on. Satan's power is in the lie, and when his lie is exposed by the truth, his plans are foiled.

When I was a boy on the farm, my dad, my brother, and I would visit our neighbor's farm to share produce and labor. The neighbor had a yappy little dog that scared the socks off me. When it came barking around the corner, my dad and brother stood their ground, but I ran. Guess who the dog chased! I escaped to the top of our pickup truck while the little dog yapped at me from the ground.

Everyone except me could see that the little dog had no power over me except what I gave it. Furthermore, it had no inherent power to throw me up on the pickup; it was my *belief* that put me up there. That dog controlled me by using my mind, my emotions, my will, and my muscles, all of which were motivated by fear. Finally I gathered up my courage, jumped off the pickup, and kicked a small rock at the mutt. Lo and behold, it ran!

Satan is like that yappy little dog: deceiving people into fearing him more than God. His power is in the lie. He is the father of lies (John 8:44) who deceives the whole world (Revelation 12:9), and consequently the whole world is under the influence of the evil one (1 John 5:19). He can do nothing about your position in Christ, but if he can deceive you into believing his lies about you and God, you will spend a lot of time on top of the pickup truck! You don't have to outshout him or outmuscle him to be free of his influence. You just have to *outtruth* him. *Believe, declare, and act upon the truth of God's Word*, and you will thwart Satan's strategy.

This concept has had a dramatic effect on my counseling. Previously when I exposed a demonic influence in a counseling situation it would turn into a power encounter. Counselees would become catatonic, run out of the room, or become suddenly disoriented, and I would attempt to take authority over the demon. My first approach was to get the demon to expose itself, then I would command it to leave. This exchange often resulted in a great deal of trauma for the counselee. Although progress was made, the episode would usually have to be repeated.

But I have learned from the Scriptures and my experience that *truth* is the liberating agent. The power of Satan is in the lie, and the power of the believer is in knowing the truth. We are to pursue *truth*, not power.

Furthermore, persons in bondage are not liberated by what I do as the pastor/counselor, but what they do with my help. It's not what *I* believe that breaks the bonds, it's what *they* believe, confess, renounce, and forgive. Notice the progressive logic of Scripture:

> You shall know the truth, and the truth shall make you free (John 8:32).

> I am the way, and the truth, and the life (John 14:6).

> But when He, the Spirit of truth, comes, He will guide you into all the truth (John 16:13).

I do not ask Thee to take them out of the world, but to keep them from the evil one.... Sanctify them in the truth; Thy word is truth (John 17:15,17).

Stand firm therefore, having girded your loins with truth (Ephesians 6:14).

Finally, brethren, whatever is true... let your mind dwell on these things (Philippians 4:8).

When God first disciplined the early church in Acts 5, He did so in a dramatic way. What was the issue: drugs, sex? No, the issue was *truth*. Peter confronted Ananias and Sapphira: "Why has Satan filled your heart to lie to the Holy Spirit?" (verse 3). God wanted the church to know that Satan the deceiver can ruin us if he can get us to believe and live a lie. That's why it is so important that we take "every thought captive to the obedience of Christ" (2 Corinthians 10:5). If I could infiltrate a church, a committee, or a person undetected, and deceive them into believing a lie, I could control their lives! That's exactly what Satan is doing, and his lie is the focus of the battle.

SETTING CAPTIVES FREE

One of the common objections to the ministry of setting captives free performed by Jesus and the apostles is the apparent lack of instruction on the subject in the epistles. Let me offer another perspective which may help clarify the issue, and let me suggest how we should confront demonic influence in our own lives and minister to others in bondage.

Prior to the cross, divinely empowered agents—such as Jesus and His specifically appointed apostles—were necessary to take authority over demonic powers in the world. But something radical happened at the cross and in the resurrection that changed the nature of spiritual conflicts forever. First, Jesus' death and resurrection triumphed over and disarmed the rulers and authorities of the kingdom of darkness (Colossians 2:15). Prior to the cross, "all authority . . . in heaven and on earth" had not yet been given to Christ. But Matthew 28:18 assures us that the resurrected Christ is now the seat of all authority. Because of the cross Satan is a defeated foe, and he has no authority over those who are in Christ. Affirming the truth of Christ's victory and Satan's defeat is the primary step to successfully combating the enemy's attempts to intimidate you and hassle you.

Second, in Christ's death and resurrection every believer is made alive with Him and is now seated with Him in the heavenlies (Ephesians 2:5,6). You no longer need an outside agent to effect authority for you; you now reside in God's special agent, Jesus Christ, who has all authority. In order to resist the devil, you need to understand and appropriate your position and authority in Christ. Freedom is your inheritance as a Christian. That's why Paul wrote:

> I pray that the eyes of your heart may be enlightened, so that you may know what is the hope of His calling, what are the riches of the glory of His inheritance in the saints, and what is the surpassing greatness of His power toward us who believe. These are in accordance with the working of the strength of His might which He brought about in Christ, when He raised Him from the dead, and seated Him at His right hand in the heavenly places, far above all rule and authority and power and dominion, and every name that is named, not only in this age, but also in the one to come (Ephesians 1:18-21).

When Satan harasses you, you may be prone to languish in the shadows of your misery, like the woman whose prayer note opened this chapter. You cry out for God to deliver you, like Jesus miraculously and instantaneously delivered the demonized people in the Gospels. But when you read through the epistles it is obvious that your deliverance has already been accomplished in Christ's work on the cross and His resurrection. That was the good news Paul was trying to convey in his prayer. Since you are with Christ in the light, you never again need to live in the shadows.

But it is your responsibility to exercise your authority and resist the devil. From your position in Christ, you must resist the devil, renounce participation in his schemes, confess sin, and forgive those who have offended you. These critical steps to freedom for yourself and those to whom you minister are the focus of Part Three of this book.

Incidentally, the woman who called herself "A Lost Sheep" finally gained God's perspective on her condition. Four years after she wrote her desperate prayer, she penned a response based on her new understanding of God's provision in Christ. Her words are based on Scripture. Allow them to shine some light into the shadows of your life.

> My Dear Lost Sheep,
>
> You ask Me where I am. My child, I am with you and I always will be. You are weak, but in Me you are strong. I love you so much that I can't let you die. I am so close that I feel everything you feel.
>
> I know what you are going through, for I am going through it with you. But I have set you free and you must stand firm. You do not need to die physically for my enemies to be gone, but be crucified with Me and I will live in you, and you shall live with Me. I will direct you in paths of righteousness. My child, I love you and I will never forsake you, for you are truly mine.
>
> —Love, God

2

Finding Your Way in the World

In the past several years I have spoken on a number of Southern California university campuses at the invitation of Campus Crusade for Christ. Fliers were distributed inviting students to attend meetings on the topic of demonic influences in the world today, but the real purpose of each meeting was to share the claims of Christ. To my surprise, several hundred students filled each auditorium. These were not fad-seeking teenagers or argumentative hecklers (although a group of Satanists did gather outside a recent meeting to chant!). Nor did they come to hear Neil Anderson, because they had no idea who I was. These people had a genuine interest in demonic influences, a subject which was scoffed at in educated circles less than 20 years ago.

While Christians have been questioning the reality of demonic influence in the church, the world has charged into the spiritual realm with reckless abandon. The Western world is experiencing a massive paradigm shift in its worldview, as best seen in the rise of the New Age movement, the acceptance of parapsychology as a science, the growing popularity of the supernatural, and the increasing visibility of Satanism in our culture. New Age mysticism, which gathered its greatest strength with the influx of Eastern religions in the 1960's, has been popularized by Shirley MacLaine (*Dancing in the Dark* and *Out on a Limb*) and a host of other celebrities in the 1980's. It's almost commonplace today to hear channelers (mediums) on radio and TV talk shows bragging about their spirit guides (demons).

But the New Age movement is not just a celebrity issue. New Age philosophy is making significant inroads into business, education, and even religion across our nation. Recently I challenged two of my students to attend, for the sake of research, a New Age conference being held two blocks from our school. When they arrived at the door and discovered the cost to be 65 dollars each, they started to walk away. But two strangers approached them saying, "We were told to give you these tickets." My wide-eyed students took the tickets and walked in.

They reported to me that one of the speakers led conference participants in a meditation exercise. He challenged everyone to imagine a spirit guide coming alongside. The speaker concluded the exercise by saying, "Now invite your spirit guide to come in." I could hardly believe it. The devil is giving altar calls just two blocks from Biola University!

THE TWO-TIER WORLDVIEW

The Western world today sees reality in two tiers (see Figure 2a). The upper tier is the transcendent world where ghosts and ghouls reside, a world which is understood through religion and mysticism. The lower tier is the empirical world, which is understood through science and the physical senses. In two-tier mentality, the spiritual world has no practical bearing on the natural world; we have excluded it from our understanding of reality. Most attempts at integrating theology and psychology include only God and humanity (fallen and redeemed) and exclude the activity of Satan and demons.

In stark contrast to the strict secularism of the West, two thirds of the inhabitants of the world hold an eastern world view. They live and operate believing that spiritual forces are an everyday reality. These people appease their gods with peace offerings and perform religious rituals to ward

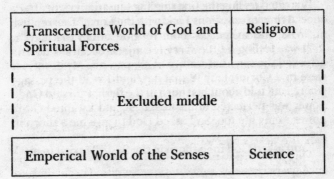

Transcendent World of God and Spiritual Forces	Religion
Excluded middle	
Emperical World of the Senses	Science

Figure 2a

off evil spirits. To the common people in Third World nations, religious practice or superstition has more practical relevance in daily life than science.

It is easy for those of us raised in the West to dismiss the Eastern worldview as inferior on the basis of the "success" of the Western world. But both are worldly systems and neither reflects biblical reality.

Between the two tiers is what Dr. Paul Hiebert calls the "excluded middle," the real world of spiritual forces active on earth. We must include the kingdom of darkness in our worldview because in reality there is no excluded middle!

To illustrate how this secular, two-tier mentality has affected the thinking of some Western Christians, let me tell you about a bright young woman named Dee, a pastor's daughter. Dee developed physical symptoms which were later diagnosed as multiple sclerosis. When I heard about Dee's condition and the prospect of her life with this debilitating disease, I felt the inner pain her parents must have felt. I prayed for Dee, but I couldn't get her off my mind. The next time I had an opportunity to see her, I took it.

"When did you first become aware of the symptoms?" I asked.

"I started feeling the first tingling sensations right after a special time of devotions I had with the Lord," Dee replied.

"What was so special about your devotions that day?"

"I was feeling a little sorry for myself because I haven't achieved the spiritual stature of my parents. My devotions were in 2 Corinthians 12 that day, and I read the passage where Paul told about his thorn in the flesh. Paul said God's power was perfected in his weakness, and I wanted God's power in my life too. So I asked God to give me a thorn in the flesh."

"You asked God for a thorn in the flesh?" I tried to mask my shock.

"Yes."

"Do you know what Paul's thorn in the flesh was?"

"Some sort of physical problem, wasn't it?"

"Well, we're not told how it was manifested, but 2 Corinthians 12:7 clearly states that it was a 'messenger of Satan,' literally an angel of Satan—a demon! Paul never asked for it. In fact, he prayed three times that it be removed. Dee, I think Satan took advantage of your unscriptural prayer and afflicted you with these symptoms. I strongly recommend that you renounce your request for a thorn in the flesh and pray that any influence by Satan be removed from your life."

Dee received my counsel and we prayed together. She began to feel better almost immediately. The symptoms disappeared and she resumed her normal activities. Several months later the symptoms began to reappear. At that time I led her through a more thorough procedure of the steps to freedom as described in Part Three of this book. Today Dee is free.

Her father's initial reaction to Dee's illness was typical of many Western Christians who perceive life through the grid of natural phenomena: "I never even considered Dee's condition to be a spiritual problem." For the same reason, some people argue that Dee's "recovery" was remission of a physical disease instead of freedom from a demonic stronghold.

We have not been taught that the spiritual world *does* impinge on the natural world. We have bought into the secular worldview of the West. Many Christians either exclude the supernatural from their worldview altogether or consign it to the transcendental tier where it will have no effect on their lives. By doing so they not only exclude God's power from their theology and practice but they also explain all human failure—even that which is induced by demonic influence, such as Dee's symptoms—as the result of psychological or natural causes.

LIVING IN THE EXCLUDED MIDDLE

The Christian worldview perceives life through the grid of Scripture, not through culture or experience. And Scripture clearly teaches that supernatural, spiritual forces are at work in the natural world. For example, approximately one-fourth of all the healings recorded in the Gospel of Mark were actually deliverances from demon activity. The woman whom Jesus healed in Luke 13:11,12 had been the victim of a "sickness caused by a spirit" for 18 years.

In addition to Dee and her symptoms, many people I have counseled came with physical problems which disappeared shortly after the demonic influence was dealt with. The most common symptoms I have seen are headaches, dizziness, and general pain throughout the body. Parallel to my experience with Dee, C. Fred Dickason in his book *Demon Possession and the Christian* tells about a client with M.S. symptoms as a result of demonization.[1] I also have a friend who shares a similar story of M.S. symptoms which disappeared when her spiritual conflict was resolved. When the symptoms revisited her several months later, she was able to deal with them and dismiss them the same day.

I'm not saying that everyone who is ill or in pain is being terrorized by a demon. That's going overboard toward the transcendental tier. But I am convinced that many Christians battle physical symptoms unsuccessfully through natural means when the essence of the problem and the solution is spiritual.

The fact that Jesus left us "in the world" (John 17:11) to wrestle against "spiritual forces of wickedness in the heavenly places" (Ephesians 6:12) is a present-day reality. Supernatural forces are at work on planet Earth. We live in the natural world, but we are involved in a spiritual war. The excluded middle is only excluded in our secularized minds, not in reality.

Getting Spiritual Without God

Over the last three decades people in the West have begun to sense that there is more to life than science has revealed and their senses have experienced—and, of course, they're right. On the surface this new hunger may sound encouraging to those of us with a Christian worldview, but in fact the same people who are disillusioned with the materialistic world are also disillusioned with established religion. Instead of turning to Christ and His church, they are filling their spiritual void with old-fashioned occultism dressed in the modern garb of parapsychology, holistic health, Eastern mysticism, and numerous cults marching under the banner of the New Age movement.

Attempting to meet spiritual needs apart from God is nothing new. Christ encountered a secularized form of Judaism during His earthly ministry which was bound to its traditions instead of to the God of Abraham, Isaac, and Jacob. The religious leaders of the day didn't recognize the Messiah as their spiritual deliverer. They perceived the oppressor to be Rome, not Satan, the god of this world. But Jesus tied the two tiers together when "the Word became flesh" (John 1:14). He came to undo the works of *Satan* (1 John 3:8), not Caesar.

Now, as then, the center of the secular worldview is self: What will *I* get out of this? Who will meet *my* needs? I'm doing *my own* thing. Even a Christian who operates in this sphere is motivated by selfish ambition and pride.

The apostle Peter is a glaring example of the struggle between self and Christ-centered living. Only moments after Peter confessed the fundamental truth that Jesus Christ is the Messiah, the Son of the living God (Matthew 16:13-16), he found himself in league with the powers of darkness. Having just blessed Peter for his noble confession, Jesus announced to him and the other disciples the suffering and death which awaited Him at Jerusalem. "And Peter took Him aside and began to rebuke Him, saying, 'God forbid it, Lord! This shall never happen to You'" (verse 22).

Jesus responded: "Get behind Me, Satan! You are a stumbling block to Me, for you are not setting your mind on God's interests, but man's" (verse 23).

Jesus' memorable rebuke seems mercilessly severe. But the fact that He identified Satan as the source of Peter's words describes precisely and appropriately the character of the advice Peter tried to give: "Save yourself at all costs. Sacrifice duty to self-interest, the cause of Christ to personal convenience." Peter's advice was satanic in principle, for Satan's primary aim is to promote self-interest as the chief end of man. Satan is called the prince of this world because self-interest rules the secular world. He is called the accuser of the brethren because he does not believe that even a child of God has a higher motive than self-service. You can almost hear him hissing, "All men are selfish at heart and have their price. Some may hold out longer than others, but in the end every man will prefer his own things to the things of God."

That's Satan's creed, and unfortunately the lives of all too many Christians validate his claims. Satan has deceived them into thinking they are serving themselves when in fact they are serving the world, the flesh, and the devil.

But the Christian worldview has a different center. Jesus confronts our humanistic, self-serving grids and offers the view from the cross. Only from this center can you escape the bondage of the one whose sole intent is "to steal, and kill, and destroy" (John 10:10).

THE VIEW FROM THE CROSS

Adam was the first mortal to entertain the notion that he could "be like God" (Genesis 3:5), which is the essence of the self-centered secularistic worldview that Satan promotes. Countless others since Adam have been seduced by Satan into believing that they are their own gods, and today the New Age movement is promoting this lie on a grand and international scale.

However, the biblical account of creation clearly establishes that only God the Creator is truly God. Adam and his ancestors are not gods; we are created beings which cannot exist apart from God. Adam became a living being when God breathed into him the breath of life. Adam was physically and spiritually alive, but he was not a god. God told him that if he ate of the tree of the knowledge of good and evil, he would surely die. But Satan told him that God didn't know what He was talking about, that eating the forbidden fruit would unlock his godlike potential. Adam ate and died—not physically at first, but spiritually. His sin separated him from God, as dramatically illustrated when God threw him out of the Garden of Eden.

Since Adam, every person coming into the world is born physically alive but spiritually dead (Ephesians 2:1). Being separated from God, man can only attempt to find meaning and purpose in life through his physical existence. He becomes his own little god, and his life is characterized by pride, self-exaltation, and independence from the God who made him. "I will determine my own purpose, establish my own identity, and live as I choose," he asserts confidently. That's the frame of reference Peter was coming from when he insisted that Jesus save Himself. The diabolical idea that man is his own god is the heartbeat of the Satan-inspired secularistic worldview and the primary link in the chain of spiritual bondage to the kingdom of darkness.

The problem with man's attempt at being his own god is that he was never designed to occupy that role. He lacks the necessary attributes to determine his own destiny. Even sinless, spiritually alive Adam in the garden of Eden wasn't equipped to be his own god, much less those of us born since then, who come into the world spiritually dead. Contrary to what the New Agers tell us, the potential to be a god never was in you, isn't in you now, and never will be in you. Being God is God's capacity alone.

If you desire to live in freedom from the bondage of the world, the flesh, and the devil, this primary link in the chain must be smashed. The secularistic, self-centered worldview which Satan and his emissaries are promoting all around you must be replaced by the perspective that Jesus introduced to His disciples in the wake of Peter's self-preserving rebuke:

> If anyone wishes to come after Me, let him deny himself, and take up his cross, and follow Me. For whoever wishes to save his life shall lose it; but whoever loses his life for My sake shall find it. For what will a man be profited if he gains the whole world and forfeits his soul? Or what will a man give in exchange for his soul? For the Son of Man is going to come in the glory of His Father with His angels, and will then recompense every man according to his deeds (Matthew 16:24-27).

The following six guidelines from Jesus' statement constitute the view from the cross. They are the foundational guidelines for those who would be free from the bondage of the world system and the devil who inspires it. Stay within the light of the victory of the cross and you will successfully find your way in a dark world.

Deny Yourself

Denying yourself is not the same as self-denial. Every student, athlete, and cult member practices self-denial, restricting himself from substances and activities which keep him from reaching his goals. But the ultimate purpose of self-denial is self-promotion: to receive a good grade, to break a record, to achieve status and recognition.

Jesus was talking about denying yourself in the essential battle of life: the scramble for the throne, the struggle over who is going to be God. Jesus doesn't enter into that battle; He's already won it. He occupies the throne and graciously offers to share it with us. But we want to be king in our lives by ourselves. Until we deny ourselves that which was never meant to be ours—the role of being God in our lives—we will never be at peace with ourselves or God, and we will never be free.

You were not designed to function independent of God, nor was your soul designed to function as a master. You will either serve God and His kingdom or Satan and his kingdom. When you deny yourself, you invite God to take the throne of your life, to occupy what is rightfully His, so that you may function as a person who is spiritually alive in Christ. Denying yourself is essential to spiritual freedom.

Pick Up Your Cross Daily

The cross we are to pick up on a daily basis is not our *own* cross but *Christ's* cross. We are closely identified with His cross, however, because we have been crucified with Christ and no longer live; Christ lives in us (Galatians 2:20). His cross provided forgiveness from what we have done and deliverance from what we were. We are forgiven because He died in our place; we are delivered because we died with Him. We are both justified and sanctified as a result of the cross.

To pick up the cross daily means to acknowledge every day that we belong to God. We have been purchased by the blood of the Lord Jesus Christ (1 Peter 1:18,19). When we pick up the cross we affirm that our identity is not based in our physical existence but in our relationship with God. We are identified as children of God (1 John 3:1-3) and our life is in Christ, who is our life (Colossians 3:3,4).

As a result of this acknowledgment we stop trying to do our own thing in order to live daily to please our heavenly Father. We stop trying to become something we aren't, and we rest in the finished work of Christ, who made us something very special.

Follow Christ

Seeking to overcome self by self-effort is a hopeless struggle. Self will never cast out self, because an independent self motivated by the flesh still wants to be God. We must follow Christ by being led by the Holy Spirit down the path of death to self. As Paul wrote: "We who live are constantly being delivered over to death for Jesus' sake, that the life of Jesus also may be manifested in our mortal flesh" (2 Corinthians 4:11).

This may sound like a dismal path to walk, but I assure you that it is not. It is a tremendous experience to be known by the Lord and to follow Him as an obedient, dependent sheep (John 10:27). The fact that we are led by the Spirit of God, even when it results in the painful experience of death to self, is our assurance of sonship (Romans 8:14). We were not designed to function independent of God. Only when we are dependent on Him and intent on following Christ are we complete and free to prove that the will of God is good, acceptable, and perfect (Romans 12:2).

Sacrifice the Lower Life to Gain
the Higher Life

If you want to save your natural life (i.e., find your identity and sense of self-worth in positions, titles, accomplishments, and possessions, and seek only worldly well-being) you will lose it. At best you can only possess these temporal values for a lifetime, only to lose everything for eternity. Furthermore, in all your efforts to possess these earthly treasures, you will fail to gain all that can be yours in Christ. Shoot for this world and that's all you'll get, and eventually you will lose even that. But shoot for the next world and God will throw in this one as a bonus. Paul made a similar statement: "Bodily discipline is only of little profit, but godliness is profitable for all things, since it holds promise for the present life and also for the life to come" (1 Timothy 4:8).

Sacrifice the Pleasure of Things to Gain the Pleasure of Life

What would you accept in trade for the fruit of the Spirit in your life? What material possession, what amount of money, what position or title would you exchange for the love, joy, peace, and patience that you enjoy in Christ? "Nothing," we all probably agree. But how does your day-to-day practice answer those questions? Where is the majority of your time, energy, and money being invested: in temporal or in eternal endeavors? All too often the chief end of fallen humanity is to be happy as animals rather than to be blessed as children of God.

Jesus discussed this very conflict with two of His closest friends, Mary and Martha (Luke 10:38-42). During Jesus' visit, Martha was caught up in material things, focusing on meal preparation and service, while Mary centered her attention on Jesus and His words. Martha's tendency was to love things and use people, but Jesus indicated that Mary had chosen "the good part" (verse 42) by loving people and using things. Victory over self comes as we learn to love people and use things, and not get those two activities mixed up.

Sacrifice the Temporal to Gain the Eternal

Possibly the greatest sign of spiritual maturity is the ability to postpone rewards. Hebrews 11:24-26 says: "By faith Moses, when he had grown up, refused to be called the son of Pharaoh's daughter; choosing rather to endure ill-treatment with the people of God than to enjoy the passing pleasures of sin; considering the reproach of Christ greater riches than the treasures of Egypt, for he was looking to the reward." It is far better to know that we are the children of God than to gain anything that the world calls valuable. Even if following Christ results in hardships in this life, He will make it right in eternity.

Satan's ultimate lie is that you are capable of being the god of your own life, and his ultimate bondage is getting you to live as though his lie is truth. Satan is out to usurp God's place in your life. And whenever you live independent of God, focusing on yourself instead of on the cross, preferring material and temporal values to spiritual and eternal values, he has succeeded. The world's solution to this conflict of identity is to inflate the ego while denying God the opportunity to take His rightful place as Lord. Satan couldn't be more pleased—that was his plan from the beginning.

3

You Have Every Right to Be Free

Lydia is a middle-aged woman who was dealt a bad hand in life right from the beginning. Memories of ritual and sexual abuse that she suffered as a young child have haunted her continually throughout her Christian life. When she came to see me her damaged self-image seemed beyond repair. As she told me her story, Lydia displayed little emotion, but her words reflected total despair.

"Who are you, Lydia? How do you perceive yourself?" I asked as she concluded.

"I'm evil," she answered stoically. "I'm just no good for anybody. People tell me I'm evil, and all I do is bring trouble."

"You're not evil," I argued. "How can a child of God be evil? Is that how you perceive yourself?" Lydia nodded.

I reached for a printed sheet of paper containing a number of statements describing who we are in Christ based on verses in the Bible and handed it to Lydia. (These statements are included in the Further Help section at the back of this book.) "I want you to read these statements aloud right now," I instructed. "They will remind you of your scriptural identity."

Lydia took the paper and began to read the first statement aloud rather haltingly: "I am th-the s-s-salt of the..." Suddenly her character changed. She looked up and sneered, "No way, you dirty son of a -----!"

It is never pleasant to see the evil one express his ugly personality through a victim like Lydia. But I took authority over him through prayer in Christ's name and led Lydia

41

through the steps to freedom. She was able to gain a new perspective of who she really is in Christ. Realizing that she is primarily the product of the work of Christ on the cross instead of the victim of her past, she was able to throw off the chains of spiritual bondage and begin living according to her true identity as a child of God.

Later she told me that the sheet of paper I asked her to read appeared to go blank as she started to read it. Was there something magical about the paper or the statements printed on it? No, it was only ink on paper. But there was something infinitely significant about Lydia realizing who she is in Christ. Satan had deceived her into believing she was worthless and evil, which was a lie. He was dead set against her reading those statements of truth about her identity as a child of God. He knew that God's truth would disarm his lie just as surely as the light disarms the darkness. And he wasn't about to give up without a fight.

Nothing is more foundational to your freedom from Satan's bondage than understanding and affirming what God has done for you in Christ and who you are as a result. We all live in accordance with our perceived identity. In fact, no one can consistently behave in a way that is inconsistent with how he perceives himself. Your attitudes, actions, responses, and reactions to life's circumstances are determined by your conscious and subconscious self-perception. If you see yourself as the helpless victim of Satan and his schemes, you will live like his victim and be in bondage to his lies. But if you see yourself as the dearly loved and accepted child of God that you really are, you will live like a child of God.

In this chapter I want to highlight several critical aspects of our identity in Christ. Many of you have already internalized the biblical truths summarized here, and others of you may find this section to be a little on the heavy side because of its doctrinal content. But I urge you not to skip over this review on your way to the more practical chapters. These concepts are foundational to your freedom from spiritual conflict as a child of God. The issue of spiritual identity and maturity in Christ is so vital that I again suggest you work through *Victory Over the Darkness* (Regal Books) in conjunction with your reading of this book.

You Are Eternally Alive and Well

You are comprised of at least two major parts: your material self and your immaterial self. On the outside you have a physical body, and on the inside you have a soul/ spirit: the ability to think, to feel, to choose (mind, emotions, and will are often collectively identified as the soul), and to relate to God (spirit). Your body is in union with your soul/spirit, and that makes you physically alive. As a Christian, your soul/spirit is in union with God as a result of your conversion, and that makes you spiritually alive.

When God created Adam, he was totally alive—physically and spiritually. But because of Adam's sin and subsequent spiritual death, every person who comes into the world is born physically alive but spiritually dead. Being separated from God, you lacked the presence and wisdom of God in your life, so you learned to live independent of God, centering your interests on yourself. This learned independence from God is referred to in Scripture as the flesh.

When you were born again, your soul/spirit was united with God and you came alive spiritually, as alive as Adam was in the garden before he sinned. As the epistle of Ephesians repeatedly declares, you are now in Christ, and Christ is in you. Since Christ who is in you is eternal, the spiritual life you have received from Him is eternal. You don't have to wait until you die to get eternal life; you possess it right now! And contrary to what Satan would like you to believe, he can't ever take eternal life away from you because he can't take Jesus away from you, who promised never to leave you or forsake you (Hebrews 13:5).

You Are Changed from Sinner to Saint

Have you ever heard a Christian refer to himself as "just a sinner saved by grace"? Have you referred to yourself that way? If you see yourself as a sinner you will sin; what would you expect a sinner to do? Your Christian life will be mediocre at best, with little to distinguish you from a non-Christian, thereby riddling you with feelings of defeat. Satan will seize that opportunity, pour on the guilt, and convince you that you are doomed to an up-and-down spiritual existence. As a defeated Christian you will confess your sin and strive to do better, but inwardly you will admit that you are just a sinner saved by grace, hanging on until the rapture.

Is that who you really are? No way! The Bible doesn't refer to believers as sinners, not even sinners saved by grace. Believers are called saints—holy ones—who occasionally sin. We become saints at the moment of salvation (justification) and live as saints in our daily experience (sanctification) as we continue to believe what God has done and as we continue to affirm who we really are in Christ. If you fail to see yourself as a child of God, you will struggle vainly to live like one, and Satan will have little trouble convincing you that you are no different from who you were before Christ and that you have no value to God or anyone else. But appropriating by faith the radical transformation of your core identity from sinner to saint will have a powerful, positive effect on your daily resistance to sin and Satan.

You Are a Partaker of the Divine Nature

Ephesians 2:1-3 describes our nature *before* we came to Christ: "You were dead in your trespasses and sins, in which you formerly walked according to the course of this world, according to the prince of the power of the air... and were by nature children of wrath." Before we became Christians our very nature was sin, and the result of our sin was death (separation from God). As such we served ourselves and Satan as a matter of course.

But at salvation God changed our very essence; we became "partakers of the divine nature, having escaped the corruption that is in the world by lust" (2 Peter 1:4). You are no longer in the flesh; you are in Christ. You had a sinful nature before your conversion, but now you are a partaker of Christ's divine nature. You are neither eternal nor divine, but you are eternally united with Christ's divinity. Paul said it this way: "You were formerly darkness, but now you are light in the Lord; walk as children of light" (Ephesians 5:8); "Therefore if any man is in Christ, he is a new creature" (2 Corinthians 5:17). In the face of Satan's accusations that we are no different, we must believe and live in harmony with the fact that we are eternally different in Christ.

The New Testament refers to the person you were before you received Christ as your old self ("old man" in the King James Version). At salvation your old self, which was motivated to live independent of God and was therefore characterized by sin, died (Romans 6:6), and your new self, motivated by your new identity in Christ and characterized by dependence on God, came to life (Galatians 2:20).

Your old self had to die in order to sever your relationship with sin which dominated it. Being a new person doesn't mean that you are sinless (1 John 1:8). But since your old self has been crucified and buried with Christ, you no longer *need* to sin (1 John 2:1). You sin when you choose to act independently of God.

You Can Be Victorious over the Flesh and Sin

Your death to sin ended your relationship with sin as master, but it did not terminate sin's existence. Sin is still alive, strong, and appealing, but its power and authority have been broken (Romans 8:2). Furthermore, your flesh, that part of you which was trained to live independently of God before you met Christ, did not die either. You still have memories, habits, conditioned responses, and thought patterns ingrained in your brain which prompt you to focus on your own interests. You are no longer *in the flesh* as your old self was; you are now *in Christ*. But you can still choose to *walk according to the flesh* (Romans 8:12,13), complying with those old urges to serve yourself instead of God. It is your responsibility to crucify the flesh (Romans 8:13) on a daily basis by learning to walk according to the Spirit (Galatians 5:16) and by repatterning your old thoughts by allowing your mind to be renewed (Romans 12:2).

Even though you are dead to sin, sin's strong appeal may still cause you to struggle with feeling that you are more alive to sin than you are to Christ. But Romans 6:1-11 teaches us that what is true of the Lord Jesus Christ is true of us in terms of our relationship to sin. God the Father allowed His Son to "be sin" (i.e., establish a relationship with sin) in order that all the sins of the world—past, present, and future—would fall on Him (2 Corinthians 5:21). When He died on the cross, our sins were on Him. But when He rose from the grave, there was no sin on Him. When He ascended to the Father, there was no sin on Him. And today, as He sits at the Father's right hand, there is no sin on Him. Since we are seated in the heavenlies in Christ, we too have died to sin.

When we find a promise in the Bible, we claim it. When we come to a commandment, we obey it. But when we read a truth, we believe it. The verses in Romans 6:1-11 are not commandments to obey; they are truths to be believed. Christ already died to sin, and because you are in Him, you have died to sin too. You cannot die to sin because you are already dead; you can only believe it. I've met many Christians who are still trying to die to sin, and their lives are miserable and fruitless as a result because they are struggling to do something that has already been done.

Notice the use of the past tense in Romans 6:1-11 (emphasis added): "We who *died* to sin" (verse 2); "All of us who *have been baptized* into Christ Jesus *have been baptized* into His death" (verse 3); "We *have been buried* with Him" (verse 4); "Our old self *was crucified* with Him, that our body of sin might be done away with, that we should no longer be slaves to sin" (verse 6); "For he who *has died* is freed from sin" (verse 7); "If we *have died* with Christ, we believe that we shall also live with Him" (verse 8). Since these verses are past tense, indicating what is already true about us, we can only believe them.

Verse 11 summarizes what we are to believe about our relationship to sin because of our position in Christ: "Even so consider yourselves to be dead to sin, but alive to God in Christ Jesus." It doesn't matter whether you feel dead to sin or not; you are to *consider* it so because it *is* so. People wrongly wonder, "What experience must I have in order for this to be true?" The only necessary experience is that of Christ on the cross, which has already happened. When we choose to believe what is true about ourselves and sin, and walk on the basis of what we believe, our right relationship with sin will work out in our experience. But as long as we put our experience before our belief, we will never fully know the freedom that Christ purchased for us on the cross.

On the basis of what Romans 6:1-11 instructs us to believe, Romans 6:12,13 tells us how to relate to sin: "Therefore do not let sin reign in your mortal body that you should obey its lusts, and do not go on presenting the members of your body to sin as instruments of unrighteousness; but present yourselves to God as those alive from the dead, and your members as instruments of righteousness to God." Sin is a sovereign master which demands service from its subjects. You are dead to sin, but you still have the capacity to serve it by putting your body at sin's disposal. It's up to you to choose whether you're going to let your body be used for sin or for righteousness. Satan, who is at the root of all sin, will take advantage of anyone who tries to remain neutral.

To illustrate, suppose your pastor asks to use your car to deliver food baskets to the needy, and a thief asks to use it to rob a bank. It's your car and you can choose to lend it however you want, for good or for evil. Which would you choose? There should be no question!

Your body is also yours to use to serve either God or sin and Satan, but the choice is up to you. That's why Paul wrote so insistently: "I urge you therefore, brethren, by the mercies of God, to present your bodies a living and holy sacrifice, acceptable to God, which is your spiritual service of worship" (Romans 12:1). Because of Christ's victory over sin, you are completely free to choose not to give yourself to obey sin as your master. It is your responsibility not to let sin reign in your mortal body.

You Can Be Free from the Power of Sin

"Not allowing sin to reign in my body sounds wonderful, Neil, but you don't know how hard my battle with sin is," you may be thinking. "I find myself doing what I shouldn't do and not doing what I should do. It's a constant struggle."

Yes, I know how hard the battle is; I've faced it myself. So did the apostle Paul. He wrote Romans 7:15-25 out of the same feelings of frustration that you experience. In this passage we discover God's path to freedom from the power of sin. I invite you to listen in as I walk through this passage with Dan, who is really struggling to overcome the power of sin in his life:

Neil: Dan, let's look at a passage of Scripture that seems to describe what you are presently experiencing. Romans 7:15 reads: "For that which I am doing, I do not understand; for I am not practicing what I would like to do, but I am doing the very thing I hate." Would you say that this verse describes you?

Dan: Exactly! I desire to do what God says is right, but sometimes I find myself doing just the opposite.

Neil: You probably identify with verse 16 as well: "But if I do the very thing I do not wish to do, I agree with the Law, confessing that it is good." Dan, how many personalities or players are mentioned in this verse?

Dan: These is only one person, and it is clearly "I."

Neil: It is very defeating when we know what we want to do, but for some reason can't do it. How have you tried to resolve this in your own mind?

Dan: Sometimes I wonder if I'm even a Christian. It seems to work for others, but not for me. Often I wonder if the Christian life is even possible or if God is really here.

Neil: If you and God were the only players in this scenario, it would stand to reason that you would either blame God or yourself for your predicament. But now look at verse 17: "So now, no longer am I the one doing it, but sin which indwells me." How many players are there now, Dan?

Dan: Apparently two, but I don't understand.

Neil: Let's read verse 18 and see if we can make some sense out of it: "For I know that nothing good dwells in me, that is, in my flesh; for the wishing is present in me, but the doing of the good is not."

Dan: I learned that verse a long time ago. It has been easy to accept the fact that I'm no good.

Neil: That's not what it says, Dan. In fact, it says the opposite. *Whatever it is that is dwelling in you* is not *you*. If I had a wood splinter in my finger it would be "nothing good" dwelling in me. But the "nothing good" isn't me; it's the splinter. It is also important to note that this "nothing good" is not even my flesh, but it is dwelling *in* my flesh. If we see only ourselves in this struggle it would be hopeless to live righteously. These passages are going to great lengths to tell us that there is a second party involved in our sin struggle whose nature is different from ours.

You see, Dan, when you and I were born, we were born under the *penalty* of sin. And we know that Satan and his emissaries are always working to keep us under that penalty. When God saved us, Satan lost that battle, but he didn't curl up his tail or pull in his fangs. He is now committed to keep us under the *power* of sin. We also know that he is going to work through the flesh, which remained after salvation.

Let's read on to see if we can learn more about how this battle is being waged: "For the good that I wish, I do not do; but I practice the very evil that I do not wish. But if I am doing the very thing I do not wish, I am no longer the one doing it, but sin which dwells in me. I find then the principle that evil is present in me, the one who wishes to do good" (verses 19-21).

Dan, can you identify from these passages the nature of that "nothing good" which indwells you?

Dan: Sure, it is clearly evil and sin. But isn't it just my own sin? When I sin I feel so guilty.

Neil: There is no question that you and I sin, but we are not "sin" as such. Evil is present in us, but we are not evil per se. This does not excuse us from sinning, because Paul wrote earlier that it is our responsibility not to let sin reign in our mortal bodies (Romans 6:12).

Do you ever feel so defeated that you just want to strike out at someone or yourself?

Dan: Almost every day!

Neil: But when you cool down, do you again entertain thoughts that are in line with your identity as a Christian?

Dan: Always, and then I feel terrible about lashing out.

Neil: Verse 22 explains this cycle: "For I joyfully concur with the law of God in the inner man." When we act out of character with who we really are, the Holy Spirit immediately brings conviction because of our union with God, and we often take it out on ourselves.

But soon our true nature expresses itself again and we are drawn back to God. It's like the frustrated wife who announces that she has had it with her husband. She wants out and couldn't care less about the bum. But after she acknowledges her pain and expresses her emotions, she softens and says, "I really love him, and I don't want a divorce. But I just don't see any other way out." That's the inner person, the true self, being expressed.

Verse 23 describes the nature of this battle with sin: "But I see a different law in the members of my body, waging war against the law of my mind, and making me a prisoner of the law of sin which is in my members." According to this passage, Dan, where is the battle being fought?

Dan: The battle appears to be in the mind.

Neil: That's precisely where the battle rages. Now if Satan can get you to think you are the only one in the battle, you will get down on either yourself or God when you sin. Let me put it this way. If a dog came along and bit you on the leg, would you beat on yourself or beat on the dog?

Dan: On the dog. But in my struggle with sin, nobody has ever told me that it's the "dog"—sin—which is inflicting the pain!

Neil: Exactly! So you beat on yourself. But I find that people eventually get tired of beating on themselves, so they walk away from God under a cloud of defeat and condemnation. Paul expressed this feeling in verse 24: "Wretched man that I am! Who will set me free from the body of this death?" He's not saying "*wicked* man that I am"; he's saying "*miserable* man that I am." He is defeated because he is not free. His attempts to do the right thing are met with defeat. He wonders, "Is there any victory?"

Verse 25 gives the answer: "Thanks be to God through Jesus Christ our Lord! So then, on the one hand I myself with my mind am serving the law of God, but on the other, with my flesh the law of sin."

Dan: I think I'm getting the picture. I've been blaming myself for my inability to live the Christian life. I see Paul frustrated about his failure, but he doesn't get down on himself. He accepts his responsibility, but he doesn't blame himself. More important, he expresses confidence by turning to God because the Lord Jesus will enable him to live above sin.

Neil: You're on the right track. Condemning yourself won't help because there is no condemnation for those who are in Christ Jesus (Romans 8:1,2). You need to understand the nature of the battle for your mind. Then you need to discover where you are losing that battle in your own life by allowing sin to reign in your body. When you discover it and deal with it, you can find freedom in Christ.

You Can Win the Battle for Your Mind

Romans 7:23 and 8:5-7 show that the center of all spiritual bondage is the mind. That's where the battle must be fought and won if you are to experience the freedom in Christ which is your inheritance. Paul wrote: "For though we walk in the flesh, we do not war according to the flesh, for the weapons of our warfare are not of the flesh, but divinely powerful for the destruction of fortresses. We are destroying speculations and every lofty thing raised up against the knowledge of God, and we are taking every thought captive to the obedience of Christ" (2 Corinthians 10:3-5).

Some fortresses ("strongholds" in the King James Version) of bad habits and sinful thought patterns were established when you learned to live your life independently of

God. Your non-Christian environment taught you to think about and respond to life in a non-Christian way, and those patterns and responses were ingrained in your mind as strongholds. But when you became a Christian, nobody pressed the "CLEAR" button in your mind. Your old fleshly habits and patterns weren't erased; they are still a part of your flesh which must be dealt with on a daily basis. Thankfully, however, you are not just a product of your past; you are a new creature in Christ (2 Corinthians 5:17), and now you are primarily the product of the work of Christ on the cross. Old strongholds can be destroyed, as outlined in Part Three of this book.

Just because you are now a Christian, don't think that Satan is no longer interested in manipulating you to his purposes through your mind. Satan's perpetual aim is to infiltrate your thoughts with his thoughts and to promote his lie in the face of God's truth. He knows that if he can control your thoughts, he can control your behavior.

But Satan is clever. He doesn't rumble in like a bull in a china shop; he slithers in like a snake in the grass (2 Corinthians 11:3). He can introduce his thoughts, tempting you to act independently of God, as if they were your own thoughts or even God's thoughts. Scripture clearly teaches that Satan can put thoughts in our minds even as he did with David (1 Chronicles 21:1), Judas (John 13:2), and Ananias (Acts 5:3).

One of my students exemplified how deceptive Satan's thoughts can be. Jay came into my office one day and said, "Dr. Anderson, I'm in trouble."

"What's the problem, Jay?"

"When I sit down to study I get prickly sensations all over my body, my arms involuntarily raise, my vision gets blurry, and I can't concentrate."

"Tell me about your walk with God," I probed.

"I have a very close walk with God," Jay boasted.

"What do you mean?"

"Well, when I leave school at noon each day, I ask God where He wants me to go for lunch. If I hear a thought that says Burger King, I go to Burger King. Then I ask Him what He wants me to eat. If the thought comes to order a Whopper, I order a Whopper."

"What about your church attendance?" I continued.

"I go every Sunday wherever God tells me to go. And for the last three Sundays God has told me to go to a Mormon church."

Jay sincerely wanted to do what God wanted him to do. But he was listening to his subjective thoughts as if they were God's voice instead of "taking every thought captive to the obedience of Christ" (2 Corinthians 10:5). In so doing he had opened himself up to Satan's activity in his life, with the result that his theológical studies were being sabotaged.

If you don't conquer Satan's temptation right at the threshold of your mind, you will begin to mull his thought over, consider it as an option, and eventually choose to act it out. Repeated acts form a habit, and if you exercise a sinful habit long enough, a stronghold will be established in your mind. Once a stronghold is established you have lost the ability to control your behavior in that area. Much more will be said about Satan's ploys of temptation and attempts to control your mind and behavior in Part Two.

How are strongholds destroyed? Patterns of negative thinking and behavior are learned, and they can be un-learned through disciplined Bible study and counseling. Some strongholds are anchored in demonic influences and spiritual conflicts from past and present mental assaults which lock their victims in bondage. These people need to be freed from the shackles of Satan's lies by God's truth. Jesus said: "You shall know the truth, and the truth shall make you free" (John 8:32). Part Three focuses on the steps to freedom based on the truth of God's Word.

When Teresa came to see me, she was a Christian young woman in bondage to self-destructive compulsive behavior, having survived a suicide attempt. Teresa had spent thou-sands of dollars and many months of her life in eating-disorder clinics and psychiatric hospitals. I met with her for three hours one day, leading her through the steps to freedom. A month later I received the following letter:

> Dear Neil:
>
> I just wanted to write and thank you for the time you spent with me last month. I guess I felt like nothing happened at the time we prayed and that perhaps nothing demonic was at the root of my problems. I was wrong. I have not had one self-destructive thought or compulsion since that day. I believe the deliverance process actually began in me through the prayers of other Christians in the months following my suicide attempt. But since I met with you, something is really different in my life, and I feel free today. I haven't cut myself in a month, and that is a true miracle!
>
> —Teresa

I hope you're sensing the fact that victory is truly available for those who are in Christ. There is a war raging, but we are on the winning side, for we are more than conquerors in Christ!

4

Confronting the Rebel Prince

One of the first persons I dealt with about spiritual conflicts and demonic influences was Daisy, a 26-year-old flower child from the 1960's. Daisy was a Christian and a university graduate, but she had severe mental and emotional problems which developed after her father divorced her mother. Within a period of five years Daisy had been institutionalized three times as a paranoid schizophrenic. After about three weeks of counseling with me, Daisy finally found the nerve to bring up the snakes in her life.

"What about the snakes?" I asked.

"Well, they crawl on me at night when I'm in bed," she confessed.

"What do you do when the snakes come?"

"I run in to my mother. But they always come back when I'm alone."

"I'll tell you what you should do," I continued. "When you're in bed and the snakes come, say out loud, 'In the name of Christ I command you to leave me.'"

"I couldn't do that," Daisy protested. "I'm not mature enough or strong enough."

"It's not a matter of your maturity; it's a matter of your position in Christ. You have as much right to resist Satan and make him leave as I do."

Daisy squirmed at the prospect. "Well, I guess I could do that," Daisy sighed, sounding like she had just agreed to take castor oil.

The next week when Daisy walked in she said, "The snakes are gone!"

"Great! Why didn't you tell me about them sooner?"

"Because I was afraid you would get them too. Now I realize that this was just another part of the lie."

Within a few months Daisy was free of demonic entanglements and was ministering in our children's department at church. If her problem had been strictly neurological or caused by a chemical imbalance, taking authority over the snakes in Jesus' name wouldn't have worked. But in Daisy's case the problem was spiritual, and five years of hospitalization and chemical treatment hadn't worked.

Before we discuss in detail the reality and present activity of Satan and his demons, you need to understand your position of authority in Christ as it relates to the spiritual realm. James wrote: "Resist the devil and he will flee from you" (James 4:7). But if you don't resist him, he doesn't have to go. Or if you just pull the covers over your head in fear and say, "O God, do something about these demonic influences," the evil spirits don't have to leave. Resisting the devil in your life is your responsibility based on the authority you possess in Christ.

CARRYING JESUS' BADGE OF AUTHORITY

Notice how Jesus equipped His disciples for ministry: "He called the twelve together, and gave them power and authority over all the demons, and to heal diseases. And He sent them out to proclaim the kingdom of God, and to perform healing" (Luke 9:1,2). Jesus knew that when His disciples began preaching the kingdom of God and healing the sick, demonic powers would kick up a fuss in opposition. So He specifically gave them power and authority over demons.

Later Jesus sent out 70 of His followers on a similar mission, and they "returned with joy, saying, 'Lord, even the demons are subject to us in Your name'" (Luke 10:17). These missionaries were spiritually in tune enough to know that demons existed and that they were a force to be reckoned with in their ministry. Jesus' followers had been eyewitnesses as the evil spirits opposed the Master, and they probably anticipated the same treatment. Perhaps they even started out on their mission with pangs of fear and doubt about encountering demonic resistance. But they came back astonished at the victory they experienced over evil spirits.

But Jesus quickly brought the issue of spiritual conflicts into perspective: "I have given you authority to tread upon serpents and scorpions, and over all the power of the enemy, and nothing shall injure you. Nevertheless do not rejoice in this, that the spirits are subject to you, but rejoice that your names are recorded in heaven" (Luke 10:19,20). Jesus sent out the 70 to preach the gospel and to heal, but all they could talk about when they came back was how they sent the demons running. "Don't be demon-centered," Jesus replied; "be kingdom-centered, be ministry-centered, be God-centered."

That's a good warning. As you learn to exercise authority over the kingdom of darkness in your life and in the lives of others, you may be tempted to see yourself as some kind of spiritual freedom fighter. You gravitate to Bible studies on Satanism, the occult, and the New Age movement, and you start looking for demons behind every door. But it's *truth* which sets you free, not the knowledge of error. You would have no authority at all if it weren't for your identity as a child of God and your position in Christ. *Who you are* must always take precedence over *what you do*.

The Right and the Ability

Jesus gave His disciples both *authority* and *power* over demons. What's the difference? Authority is the *right* to rule; it's a positional issue. A policeman has the right to stop traffic at an intersection because of the position of authority represented by his badge. Similarly, Jesus gave His disciples His badge to carry. They had the right to rule over the demons because of their position as followers of the One to whom all authority in heaven and on earth has been given (Matthew 28:18).

In contrast, power is the *ability* to rule. A policeman may have the authority to stop traffic, but he doesn't have the physical ability to do so. If he tries to stop traffic by his own power, he will probably get run over. However, if you move a 20-foot-square cement block into the middle of the intersection, it may not have any authority to make cars stop, but it certainly has the ability to do so!

No good manager would delegate *responsibility* to his underlings without also delegating *authority* to them and equipping them with the ability to get the job done. Jesus charged His disciples with the *responsibility* to proclaim the kingdom of God. Had He not also given them *authority and power* in the spirit world, the demons would have just scoffed at their feeble attempts and sent them running for cover (as they did the seven sons of Sceva in Acts 19).

You may think, as Daisy did, that you're not mature enough to resist demonic interference in your life. You somehow imagine that the enemy is more powerful than you are. The truth is that, while in yourself you don't have the ability to resist Satan and his demons, *in Christ you do*. The Israelites looked at Goliath fearfully and said, "We can't fight him." But young David looked at Goliath and said, "Who is this uncircumcised Philistine, that he should taunt the armies of the living God?" (1 Samuel 17:26), then blew him away with his slingshot. The army saw Goliath in relation to themselves and trembled; David saw Goliath in relation to God and triumphed. When you encounter the spiritual enemies of your soul, remember: You plus Jesus equals a majority.

People often assume that I have some degree of success at confronting demonic powers because of my education, calling, or strength of personality. That's not true at all. A little child and an aged grandmother in Christ have the same authority in the spiritual world that I do. We are to "glory in Christ Jesus and put no confidence in the flesh" (Philippians 3:3).

Pulling Rank

It was an eye-opening experience for the disciples to discover that "the demons are subject to us in Your name" (Luke 10:17). "Subject" (*hupotasso*) is a military term meaning "to arrange under." It pictures a group of soldiers snapping to attention and following precisely the orders of their commanding officer.

Perhaps the disciples suffered under the same misconception which blinds many Christians today. We see God and His kingdom on one side and Satan and his kingdom on the other side. Both kingdoms seem to be very powerful, and here we are, stuck in the middle between the two, like the rope in a tug of war. On some days God seems to be winning, and on other days the devil appears to have the upper hand. And we don't seem to have anything to say about who wins the battle.

But the disciples came back from their mission with a new perspective, a true perspective. Spiritual authority is not a tug-of-war on a horizontal plane; it is a vertical chain of command. Jesus Christ has all authority in heaven and on earth (Matthew 28:18); He's at the top. He has given His authority and power to His servants to be exercised in His name (Luke 10:17); we're underneath Him. And Satan and his demons? They're at the bottom, subject to the authority Christ has invested in us. They have no more right to rule your life than a buck private has to order a general to clean the latrine.

Why, then, does the kingdom of darkness exert such negative influence in the world and in the lives of Christians? In a word, the lie. Satan is not an equal power with God; he is a vanquished foe. But if he can deceive you into believing that he has more power and authority than you do, you will live as if he does! You have been given authority over the kingdom of darkness, but if you don't believe it and exercise it, it's as if you didn't have it.

I experienced this contrast during a counseling session with a severely demonized woman. During the session, the woman—who was big and husky—suddenly rose from her chair and walked toward me with eyes blazing and lips snarling. At that point I was glad that the weapons of our warfare are not of the flesh, because I would have had a difficult time defending myself against a demonized person of her size.

Instead, I spoke these words based on 1 John 5:18—not to the woman, because she was blanked out at the time, but to the evil spirit controlling her: "I'm a child of God, and the evil one can't touch me. Sit down right now." She stopped in her tracks and returned to her chair. Had I not exercised my authority in Christ, fear would have controlled me and some kind of power encounter would have ensued. But by taking a stand in Christ's name I neutralized the demon's hollow show of power and was able to minister the steps of freedom to the woman.

The episode was merely a demonic scare tactic designed to make me respond in fear. But "the weapons of our warfare are not of the flesh" (2 Corinthians 10:4). When Satan tries to incite fear, we are to maintain our position in Christ and exhibit the fruit of the Spirit, which includes the self-control we need in order to avoid responding in fear (Galatians 5:23).

JESUS' BADGE IN THE CONTEMPORARY WORLD

"That's all well and good for the 12 and the 70 who were equipped with authority and then sent out by Jesus," you may be thinking. "But we live in another dispensation. I see the conferring of authority in the Gospels, but is it also present in the epistles? Do we enjoy the same claim to Christ's authority in the spiritual realm as those who were personally sent out by Him?"

Absolutely! In fact, because of the death, resurrection, and ascension of Christ, and the subsequent outpouring of the Holy Spirit, we have an even greater advantage in spiritual warfare than the first disciples did. They were *with* Christ (Mark 3:14,15) but we are *in* Christ. That was Paul's great news in the opening lines of his letter to the church at Ephesus. Notice how many times he mentions our position in Christ (emphasis added):

> Blessed be the God and Father of our Lord Jesus Christ, who has blessed us with every spiritual blessing in the heavenly places *in Christ*, just as He chose us *in Him* before the foundation of the world (verses 3,4). ...To the praise of the glory of His grace, which He freely bestowed on us *in the Beloved*. *In Him* we have redemption through His blood (verses 6,7)....He made known to us the mystery of His will, according to His kind intention which He purposed *in Him* with a view to an administration suitable to the fulness of times, that is, the summing up of all things *in Christ* (verses 9,10)....*In Him* also we have obtained an inheritance...to the end that we who were the first to hope *in Christ* should be to the praise of His glory. *In Him*, you also, after listening to the message of truth, the gospel of your salvation—having also believed, you were sealed *in Him* with the Holy Spirit of promise (verses 10-13).

Paul wanted to make sure that nobody missed his point. Ten times in the first 13 verses he reminded us that everything we have is the result of our intimate, personal relationship with the resurrected Christ and His indwelling Spirit.

Having firmly established the reality of our position in Christ, Paul expressed his heart's desire for Spirit-filled believers in this prayer:

I pray that the eyes of your heart may be enlightened, so that you may know what is the hope of His calling, what are the riches of the glory of His inheritance in the saints, and what is the surpassing greatness of His power toward us who believe. These are in accordance with the working of the strength of His might which He brought about in Christ, when He raised Him from the dead, and seated Him at His right hand in heavenly places (Ephesians 1:18-20).

Why did Paul pray that our inner eyes would be opened? Because our problem with identity and self-perception as Christians is not that we aren't in Christ; it's that we don't *see* it or *perceive* it; we're just not conscious of it. And when we don't understand who we are, we don't experience the freedom and fruitfulness which is intrinsic to our identity. Furthermore, Paul suggests that our problem with authority in the spiritual world is not that we aren't tapped into the surpassing greatness of Christ's power; it's that we just don't see it. And as long as we fail to perceive our access to Christ's authority over the kingdom of darkness, we will fail to exercise that authority in our lives, and we will live in bondage.

The Depth and Breadth of Authority

In Ephesians 1:19-23 Paul gives us a peek at the dynamic source of our authority in Christ. He explains that the authority at our disposal flows from the reservoir of power which raised Jesus Christ from the dead and seated him at the Father's right hand. That power source is so dynamic that Paul used four different Greek words in verse 19 to describe it: "power" (*dunameos*), "working" (*energeian*), "strength" (*kratous*), and "might" (*ischuos*). Behind the resurrection of the Lord Jesus Christ lies the mightiest work of power recorded in the Word of God. And the same power which raised Christ from the dead and defeated Satan is the power available to us to defeat the works of Satan in our daily lives.

Paul also wants to open our eyes to the expansive scope of Christ's authority, which is "far above all rule and authority and power and dominion, and every name that is named, not only in this age, but also in the one to come" (Ephesians 1:21). Think about the most powerful and influential political or military leaders in the world, good and bad. Imagine the most feared terrorists, crime kingpins, and drug barons. Think about the notorious figures of the past and present who have blighted society with their diabolical misdeeds. Think about Satan and all the powers of darkness marshaled under his command. Jesus' authority is not only above all these human and spiritual authorities past, present, and future, but He is *far* above them. There's no comparison at all—it's not even close! And His authority is at our disposal to live in freedom and victory over demonic intrusion and influence.

This passage does not teach that we have authority over all diseases as the apostles did. We can exercise authority over demonically induced sickness, but to infer from these verses that we are able to exercise authority over germs, viruses, and bacteria is questionable at best. Our authority seems limited to the spiritual realm.

Authority Conferred

Another eye-opening truth which Paul wrote about in Ephesians 1 and 2 concerns the conferring of Christ's authority on "us who believe" (1:19). When and where did this happen? Paul has already explained that God's supreme act of power and authority occurred when He raised Christ from the dead and seated Him in the heavenlies far above all other authorities (1:19-21). After parenthetically alluding to the sinful state in which we existed prior to salvation (2:1-3), Paul continued his central theme of Christ's authority as it relates to us: "God, being rich in mercy, because of

His great love with which He loved us, even when we were dead in our transgressions, made us alive together with Christ (by grace you have been saved), and raised us up with Him, and seated us with Him in the heavenly places, in Christ Jesus" (2:4-6).

Paul wanted us to see that when Christ was raised from the dead (1:20), those of us who have believed in Him were also resurrected from our condition of spiritual death and made alive "together with Christ" (2:5,6). The resurrection of Christ from the tomb and our resurrection from spiritual death happened at the same time. It's only logical that the head (Christ) and the body (His church) should be raised together.

Furthermore, when God seated Christ at His right hand and conferred on Him all authority (Ephesians 1:20,21), He also seated us at His right hand and conferred on us through Christ all authority (2:6) because we are "together with Christ" (2:5). All of this happened at a point in time, at the historical resurrection and ascension of Jesus (about 29 A.D.), "when we were dead in our transgressions" (2:5). The moment you receive Christ, you take possession of what God did for you 2000 years ago. Your identity as a child of God and your authority over spiritual powers are not things you *are* receiving or *will* receive at some time in the future; you have them right now. You are a spiritually-alive child of God *right now*. You are seated in the heavenlies with Christ *right now*. You possess all power and authority over the kingdom of darkness *right now*.

Paul also related this life-changing truth in his letter to the Colossians: "In Him [Christ] you have been made complete, and He is the head over all rule and authority" (Colossians 2:10). Notice again that the action is past tense: We *have been* made complete. When? At the death, resurrection, and ascension of Jesus Christ. And since Christ is the God-appointed head over all rule and authority, and since we are seated with Him in the heavenlies, we are privileged to exercise His rule and authority.

Paul mentioned something else in Colossians 2 which happened at the death, resurrection, and ascension of Christ: "He...disarmed the rulers and authorities [and] made a public display of them, having triumphed over them through Him" (verse 15). Not only were you made alive in Christ 2000 years ago, but Satan was also disarmed and defeated 2000 years ago. His defeat is not pending, nor is it future; it has already happened.

If Satan is already disarmed, why don't we experience more victory in our lives? Here's that word again: the lie. Satan roams around like a hungry lion, looking and sounding ferocious. In reality his fangs have been removed and he has been declawed, but if he can deceive you into believing that he can chew you up and spit you out, he can control your behavior, which is just what he wants to do. In reality he is just faking Christians into defeat!

The very reason Christ conferred His authority on us was to demonstrate to the kingdom of darkness who is really in control in this world. Later in Ephesians Paul wrote: "To me, the very least of all saints, this grace was given, to preach to the Gentiles the unfathomable riches of Christ, and to bring to light what is the administration of the mystery which for ages has been hidden in God, who created all things; in order that the manifold wisdom of God might now be made known through the church to the rulers and authorities in the heavenly places" (Ephesians 3:8-10).

How are we doing at making Christ's victory known to "the rulers and authorities in heavenly places"? In many quarters, not very well. Some of us are still saying, "What rulers and authorities?" We're not sure that demons even exist. How are we ever going to get our job done in the world if we don't believe what God says about the kingdom of darkness? Others of us are cowering in the corner pleading, "O God, please help us! The devil is roaring at us!" And God responds, "I've done all I'm going to do. I defeated and disarmed Satan at the cross. I conferred all authority on you in Christ. Now open your eyes. Realize who you are and start demonstrating the authority you already possess."

Do You Have What It Takes?

What does it take to effectively exercise Christ's authority over spiritual powers? Can any Christian do so regardless of his level of spiritual maturity? If so, why aren't we more consistent in demonstrating our authority over Satan's kingdom?

I believe there are at least four qualifications for demonstrating authority over rulers and authorities in the spiritual realm.

1. *Belief.* Imagine a rookie traffic cop approaching a busy intersection to direct traffic for the first time. They told him at the academy that all he had to do was step into the street and hold up his hand and the cars would stop, but he's not so sure. He stands on the curb, tweets his whistle weakly, and sort of waves at an oncoming car, which just roars by him. His authority is diminished by his lack of confidence.

Now imagine a seasoned officer coming on the scene. He sizes up the situation, steps into the street carefully but confidently, gives a blast on his whistle, and stretches out his hand—and the cars stop. There's no doubt in his mind that he's in control in that intersection because he has a settled belief in his authority.

In the spiritual realm, if you don't believe you have authority, you're not going to exercise it. If your belief is weak, your expression of it will also be weak and ineffective. But if you grasp with confidence the authority that Christ has conferred upon you, you will exercise it with confidence.

I received an interesting phone call one night from a youth pastor whose belief in his authority was being put to the test. He was visiting at the home of one of his young people while the parents were out bowling. It was a Christian family, but an older brother in the home had been living a lie. He was deceiving his family members and being deceived.

"Dr. Anderson, I was sitting here visiting with the kid from my group and his little sister when we sensed an evil presence in the room. It scared us all, so we decided to check out the rest of the house. One room we went into felt 20 degrees colder than the rest of the house. I knew something was very wrong."

"What did you do?" I asked.

"I said out loud, 'All right, I know you're here. Show yourself to us.' Suddenly a picture on the wall turned 90 degrees. That's when I decided I had better call you."

My young friend's belief in his authority had suddenly worn thin. If you ever challenge an evil spirit like he did, you need to be able to exercise your authority in Christ and resolve the conflict.

I went to the house the next night and met with the whole family, including the boy whose lying ways had opened the door for demonic activity. We prayed together, and the father, as head of the household, took authority over their home.

For two days there was no evidence of an evil presence. Then one night the enemy apparently decided to test the family's authority. The little girl woke up in the middle of the night terrified. She saw an eerie light in the hallway shining under her bedroom door. Her parents were asleep across the hall and she wanted to go to them, but she was afraid to open the door. Finally, remembering our prayer time a few nights earlier, she exercised her belief and opened the door. As soon as she did the light was gone, never to return.

You may consider yourself just a "rookie" at stopping the devil's traffic in your life. But Jesus Christ is a seasoned veteran, and you're in Him. Build your faith in your authority by studying how Jesus operated against the powers of darkness in the Gospels and how we are commanded to do so in the epistles.

2. *Humility*. Humility doesn't mean that you're always looking for a rock to crawl under because you feel unworthy to do anything. I define humility as confidence which is properly placed. In exercising our authority, humility is placing confidence in Christ, the source of our authority, instead of in ourselves. Jesus didn't shrink back from exercising His authority, but He showed tremendous humility because He did everything according to what His Father told Him to do.

Pride says, "I resisted the devil all by myself." False humility says, "God resisted the devil; I did nothing." True humility says, "I resisted the devil by the grace of God." Apart from Christ we can do *nothing* (John 15:5), but that doesn't mean we're not supposed to do *something*. We exercise authority humbly in His strength and in His name.

3. *Boldness*. A Spirit-filled Christian is characterized by a true, godly sense of courage and boldness in spiritual warfare. On the eve of taking authority over the Promised Land, Joshua was challenged four times to be strong and courageous (Joshua 1:6,7,9,18). When the early church prayed about their mission of sharing the gospel in Jerusalem, "the place where they had gathered together was shaken, and they were all filled with the Holy Spirit, and began to speak the word of God with boldness" (Acts 4:31). Spirit-inspired boldness is behind every successful advance in the church today.

The opposite of boldness is cowardice, fear, and unbelief. Notice what God thinks about these characteristics:

> I am the Alpha and Omega, the beginning and the end. I will give to the one who thirsts from the spring of the water of life without cost. He who overcomes shall inherit these things, and I will be his God and he

will be My son. But for the cowardly and unbelieving and abominable and murderers and immoral persons and sorcerers and idolaters and all liars, their part will be in the lake that burns with fire and brimstone, which is the second death (Revelation 21:6-8).

That's pretty serious—cowards lined up at the lake of fire alongside murderers, sorcerers, and idolaters! It should serve to motivate us to exercise authority with boldness (2 Timothy 1:7).

A lot of Christians I meet fear the dark side of the spiritual world. I've even had Talbot students tell me, "I'd like to take your class on spiritual conflicts, but I'm afraid to talk about demons." It's true that a little knowledge can be a dangerous and frightful thing, but a growing knowledge of the truth can be liberating. Typically, after a group of students has completed the course, a few will say, "I used to be afraid of that stuff, but now I know who I am in Christ, and I'm not afraid anymore." That's exactly the perception we should have.

4. *Dependence.* The authority we're talking about here is not an independent authority. We don't charge out on our own initiative like some kind of evangelical ghostbusters to hunt down the devil and engage him in combat. God's primary call is for each of us to focus on the ministry of the kingdom: loving, caring, preaching, teaching, praying, etc. However, when demonic powers challenge us in the course of pursuing this ministry, we deal with them on the basis of our authority in Christ and our dependence on Him. Then we carry on with our primary task.

Nor is the authority of the believer an authority to be exercised over other believers. We are to be "subject to one another in the fear of Christ" (Ephesians 5:21). There is a God-established authority on earth which governs the social structures of government, work, home, and church (Romans 13:1-7). It is critically important that we submit to these governing authorities unless they require us to commit a moral offense toward God.

The Bottom Line: Freedom

When we boldly and humbly exercise the authority that Christ has conferred upon us over the spiritual realm, we experience the freedom from bondage which Christ promised (John 8:32). It's usually a freedom that secular counseling can't produce, as a friend of mine discovered.

Christy, a young woman, came to my friend Barry because of the horrible abuse she suffered growing up. Barry dealt with Christy on family and social issues, and Christy complied with his suggestions. But she didn't get any better. After working with Christy for nearly four years, Barry brought her to me.

"Tell me about your childhood friends, Christy," I probed.

"The only other girl on our block lived across the street from me, so we were friends."

"What was her family like?"

Christy lowered her eyes. "Her mother did strange things in their home," she almost whispered.

"Did these strange things involve candles and sacrifices, sometimes even killing animals?"

"Yeah."

By this time Barry's eyes were as big as silver dollars. In nearly four years of counseling she had never told him that a witch lived across the street from her as a child. He didn't know enough to ask these questions, and she hadn't volunteered this information. Most people won't talk about these things if they sense the counselor won't receive it properly.

"Were you ever required to take off your clothes during these rituals?" Christy nodded. "And were there others there, men and women, who took off their clothes and performed sexual acts with you and each other?" Again she nodded.

Christy's neighbor finally moved away. But every night the witch appeared to her in her room and talked with her. I led her through the steps to freedom, and she exercised her authority in Christ and dismissed the evil influence from her life. It came back occasionally, and sometimes Christy failed to stand against it because she was "just tired of fighting the battle." But when she stood her ground on Christ's authority, she was free.

Satan can do nothing about your position in Christ. But if he can, he will cloud your perspective and thus diminish your faith and dull your effectiveness in the spiritual battle. I want to echo Paul's prayer in Ephesians 1. I pray that your eyes will be opened so you can see and understand the authority and power that Christ has extended to you as a believer.

5

Jesus Has You Covered

I received the following letter during a weeklong conference I was conducting on spiritual conflicts. Frances' struggle vividly captures the nature of the spiritual conflict which entangles many Christians:

Dear Dr. Anderson:

I attended your Sunday sessions, but while waiting to talk to you after the Sunday evening meeting I suddenly felt ill. I was burning up like I had a fever, and I got so weak I thought I was going to faint. So I went home.

I need help. I've had more trouble in my life since I became a Christian than I ever had before. I've overdosed on alcohol and drugs so many times I can't count them. I've cut myself several times with razor blades, sometimes very seriously. I have thoughts and feelings and ideas of suicide weekly, like stabbing myself through the heart. I'm a slave to masturbation; I'm out of control, and I don't know how to stop.

On the outside I appear very normal. I have a good job, and I live with an outstanding family in our community. I even work with junior highers at my church. But I can't really explain my relationship with God anymore. I've been seeing a psychiatrist for two years. Sometimes I think I'm this way because of a messed-up childhood, or maybe I was born this way.

How can I tell if my problems are in my mind, or the result of sin and disobedience against God, or the evidence of demonic influence? I would like to talk to you during the conference. But I don't want to try any more remedies that don't work.

—Frances

The confusion in Frances' mind is a clear tip-off that her problem is the result of demonic influence. I met with her that week, and she was as miserable, frustrated, and defeated as she sounds in her letter. She wanted to serve God with all her heart, and she had as much access to the power and authority to resist Satan as you or I do. But she was getting slammed around like a hockey puck by the powers of darkness because she didn't understand her authority or her protection in Christ.

Once Frances began to realize that she was not powerless or defenseless in the battle, and that she could make choices to change her situation, the chains dropped off and she walked free. Her freedom not only changed her life dramatically, but it also affected many others around her for good.

GETTING INVOLVED IN GOD'S PROTECTION

Have you experienced the reality of Frances' statement: "I've had more trouble in my life since I became a Christian than I ever had before"? When you become a child of God, you gain an enemy you didn't have before. In your B.C. days (before Christ), the god of this world didn't bother with you because you were already part of his kingdom. His goal was to keep you there by blinding you to God's provision for your salvation (2 Corinthians 4:3,4). But when you came to life in Christ, Satan didn't curl up his tail and pull in his fangs. He is still committed to foul up your life through his deception to "prove" that Christianity doesn't work, that God's Word isn't true, and that nothing really happened when you were born again.

"So what's the benefit of being a Christian? Who in his right mind would want to sign up for a life of trouble?" you may wonder. In reality, it doesn't need to be a life of trouble. You don't have to be a defenseless hockey puck at the mercy of Satan and his demons. God has already supplied the protection you need to ward off any and every attack in the spiritual realm. You just need to know what God has provided and to apply it to your own experience.

Some Christians are a little paranoid about evil powers, suspecting that demons lurk around every corner just waiting to possess them. That's an unfounded fear. Our relationship to demonic powers in the spiritual realm is a lot like our relationship to germs in the physical realm. We know that germs are all around us: in the air, in the water, in our food, in other people, even in us. But do you live in constant fear of catching some disease? No—unless you're a hypochondriac! You know enough about wellness to eat the right foods, get enough rest, and keep yourself and your possessions clean. If you happen to catch a cold or get the measles, you simply deal with it and go on with your life.

It's the same in the spiritual realm. Demons are like little invisible germs looking for someone to infect. We are never told in Scripture to be afraid of them. You just need to be aware of their reality and commit yourself to live a righteous life in spite of them. Should you come under attack, deal with it and go on with life. Remember: The only thing big about a demon is its mouth. Demons are habitual liars. In Jesus Christ the Truth, you are equipped with all the authority and protection you need to deal with anything they throw at you.

The Christian's Magna Charta of protection is Ephesians 6:10-18. The first thing you should see in this passage about receiving God's protection is that our role is not passive. God requires us to be active participants in the spiritual defense that He has provided for us. Notice how often we are commanded to take an active role (emphasis added):

> Finally, *be strong* in the Lord and in the strength of His might. *Put on* the full armor of God, that you may

be able to *stand firm* against the schemes of the devil. For our struggle is not against flesh and blood, but against the rulers, against the powers, against the world forces of this darkness, against the spiritual forces of wickedness in the heavenly places. Therefore, *take up* the full armor of God, that you may *be able* to *resist* in the evil day, and having done everything, to *stand firm* (verses 10-13).

You may be wondering, "If my position in Christ is secure and my protection is found in Him, why do I have to get actively involved? Can't I just rest in Him and let Him protect me?" That's like a soldier saying, "Our country is a major military power. We have the most advanced tanks, planes, missiles, and ships in the world. Why should I bother with wearing a helmet, standing guard, or learning how to shoot a gun? It's much more comfortable to stay in camp while the tanks and planes fight the war." When the enemy troops infiltrate, guess who will be one of the first soldiers to get picked off!

God, our "commanding officer," has provided everything we need to secure victory over the evil forces of darkness. But He says, "I've prepared a winning strategy and designed effective weapons. But if you don't do your part by staying on active duty, you're likely to become a casualty." In her classic book *War on the Saints*, Jessie Penn-Lewis stated: "The chief condition for the working of evil spirits in a human being, apart from sin, is passivity, in exact opposition to the condition which God requires from His children for His working in them."[1] You can't expect God to protect you from demonic influences if you don't take an active part in His prepared strategy.

DRESSED FOR SUCCESS

A primary element in our protection is the armor that God has provided for us and instructed us to put on. Paul wrote:

Stand firm therefore, having girded your loins with truth, and having put on the breastplate of righteousness, and having shod your feet with the preparation of the gospel of peace; in addition to all, taking up the shield of faith with which you will be able to extinguish all the flaming missiles of the evil one. And take the helmet of salvation, and the sword of the Spirit, which is the word of God (Ephesians 6:14-17).

When we put on the armor of God we are really putting on Christ (Romans 13:12-14). And when we put on Christ we take ourselves out of the realm of the flesh, where we are vulnerable to attack, and we place ourselves within the dominion of Christ, where the evil one cannot touch us. Satan has nothing in Christ (John 14:30), and to the extent that we put on Christ, the evil one cannot touch us (1 John 5:18). He can only touch that which is on his own level. That's why we are commanded, "Make no provision for the flesh" (Romans 13:14), meaning "Don't live on Satan's level."

Armor You Have Already Put On

It would appear from the verb tenses in Ephesians 6:14,15 that three of the pieces of armor—belt, breastplate, and shoes—are already on you: "having girded...", "having put on...", "having shod..." These pieces of armor represent the elements of your protection made possible when you receive Jesus Christ and in which you are commanded to stand firm. The Greek tense of "having" signifies that the action it refers to was completed before we were commanded to stand firm. That's the logical way a soldier would prepare for action: He would put on his belt, breastplate, and shoes before attempting to stand firm. Likewise, we are to put on the full armor of God after having already put on Christ.

The belt of truth. Jesus said, "I am the truth" (John 14:6). And because Christ is in you, the truth is in you. However, continuing to choose truth is not always easy. Since Satan's primary weapon is the lie, your belt of truth (which holds the other pieces of body armor in place) is continually being attacked. If he can disable you in the area of truth, you become an easy target for his other attacks.

You stand firm in the truth by relating everything you do to the truth of God's Word. If a thought comes to mind which is not in harmony with God's truth, dismiss it. If an opportunity comes along to say or do something which compromises or conflicts with truth, avoid it. Adopt a simple rule of behavior: If it's the truth, I'm in; if it's not the truth, count me out.

When you learn to live in the truth on a daily basis, you will grow to love the truth because you have nothing to hide. You never have to cover up to God or anyone else; everything you do is in the light. Furthermore, when you live in the truth you dislodge the lies of Satan, the father of lies (John 8:44). Remember that if Satan can deceive you into believing a lie, he can control your life in that area.

Jesus prayed, "I do not ask Thee to take them out of the world, but to keep them from the evil one" (John 17:15). How? "Sanctify them in the truth; Thy Word is truth" (verse 17). You will only dislodge Satan's lies in the light of God's revelation, and not by human rationalization.

The breastplate of righteousness. When you put on Christ at salvation you are justified before our holy God. It's not *your* righteousness but Christ's (1 Corinthians 1:30; Philippians 3:8,9). So when Satan aims an arrow at you by saying, "You're not good enough to be a Christian," you can respond with Paul, "Who will bring a charge against God's elect? God is the one who justifies" (Romans 8:33). Your righteousness in Christ is your protection against Satan's accusations about your worth to a holy God.

Even though we rejoice in our position of righteousness in Christ, we are well aware of our deeds of unrighteousness when we think, say, or do something apart from God. We are saints who occasionally sin. Standing firm in our righteousness involves understanding and applying the principle of confession.

God's remedy for sin is stated in 1 John 1:9: "If we confess our sins, He is faithful and righteous to forgive us our sins and to cleanse us from all unrighteousness." Confession is different from saying "I'm sorry" or asking forgiveness. To confess (*homologeo*) means to acknowledge or to agree. Suppose a father catches his son throwing a rock at a car. Dad says, "You threw a rock at a car, and that was wrong." If the boy responds, "I'm sorry, Dad," has he confessed? Not really. He may also say, "Please forgive me, Dad," but has he actually confessed yet? No. He hasn't confessed until he agrees with his dad, "I threw a rock at a car; I was wrong."

When you sin you may feel sorry, but feeling sorry or even telling God you're sorry isn't confession. You confess your sin when you say what God says about it: "I entertained a lustful thought, and that's a sin"; "I treated my spouse unkindly this morning, and that was wrong"; "pride motivated me to seek that board position, and pride doesn't belong in my life."

Satan will make confession as difficult for you as he can. He will try to convince you that it's too late for confession, that God has already erased your name out of the book of life. That's another one of his big lies. You're in Christ; you're already forgiven. You are the righteousness of God in Christ (2 Corinthians 5:21), and He will never leave you. Your relationship with God and your eternal destiny are not at stake when you sin, but your daily victory is. Your confession of sin clears the way for the fruitful expression of righteousness in your daily life. We should be like Paul, who said, "I also do my best to maintain always a blameless conscience both before God and before men" (Acts 24:16).

The shoes of peace. When you receive Christ you are united with the Prince of Peace. You have positional peace with

God right now (Romans 5:1), but the peace of Christ must also rule in your heart, and that is possible only when you let the Word of Christ richly dwell in you (Colossians 3:15,16).

The shoes of peace become protection against the divisive schemes of the devil when you act as a peacemaker among believers (Romans 14:19). Peacemakers bring people together by promoting fellowship and reconciliation. Too many Christians require common doctrine as the basis for fellowship. And it is true that if we don't think the same and believe the same, there is friction between us instead of peace. But common doctrine isn't the basis for fellowship; common heritage is. We're all children of God, and that's enough to bring us together in peace. If you wait to receive someone until you agree perfectly on every point of doctrine, you'll be the loneliest Christian on earth. Instead of insisting on the unity of the mind, preserve the unity of the Spirit by taking the initiative to be the peacemaker in your relationships (Matthew 5:9; Ephesians 4:3). We have the promise that "the God of peace will soon crush Satan under your feet" (Romans 16:20).

The Rest of the Wardrobe

Paul mentions three more pieces of armor that we must take up to protect ourselves from Satan's attack: the shield of faith, the helmet of salvation, and the sword of the Spirit, which is the Word of God. The first three are established by our position in Christ; the last three help us continue to win the battle.

The shield of faith. Contrary to popular perception, there is nothing mystical about faith. Biblical faith is simply what you believe about God and His Word. The more you know about God and His Word, the more faith you will have. The less you know, the smaller your shield will be and the easier it will be for one of Satan's fiery darts to reach its target. If you want your shield of faith to grow large and protective, your knowledge of God and His Word must increase (Romans 10:17).

These flaming missiles from Satan are nothing more than smoldering lies, burning accusations, and fiery temptations bombarding our minds. When a deceptive thought, accusation, or temptation enters your mind, meet it head-on with what you know to be true about God and His Word. How did Jesus deflect the missiles of Satan's temptation? By shielding Himself with statements from the Word of God. Every time you memorize a Bible verse, listen to a sermon, or participate in a Bible study, you increase your knowledge of God and enlarge your shield of faith.

The helmet of salvation. Should your shield of faith be a little leaky and your daily victory elusive, be confident that the helmet of salvation guarantees your eternal victory. In the metaphor of armor, the helmet also secures coverage for the most critical part of your anatomy: your mind, where spiritual battles are either won or lost. As you struggle with the world, the flesh, and the devil on a daily basis, stand firm knowing that your salvation does not come and go with your success or failure in spiritual battle; your salvation is your eternal possession. You are a child of God, and nothing can separate you from the love of Christ (Romans 8:35).

People experiencing spiritual conflict tend to question their salvation or doubt their identity in Christ. Satan may disrupt your daily victory, but he can do nothing to disrupt your position in Christ. However, if he can get you to believe that you are not in Christ, you will live as though you are not in Christ, even though you are secure in Him.

The Christian warrior wears the helmet of salvation in the sense that he is the receiver and possessor of deliverance, clothed and armed in the victory of his Head, Jesus Christ. Satan is the ruler of this world, and the whole world is in his power (John 12:31; 1 John 5:19). Therefore we are still in his territory as long as we are present in our physical bodies. But since we are joined to the Lord Jesus Christ, the devil has no legitimate claim on us, for Christ has "delivered us from the domain of darkness, and transferred us to the kingdom of His beloved Son" (Colossians 1:13). The helmet of our position in Christ assures us of ultimate victory over Satan.

The sword of the Spirit. The Word of God is the only offensive weapon mentioned in the list of armor. Since Paul used *rhema* instead of *logos* for "word" in Ephesians 6:17, I believe Paul is referring to the spoken Word of God instead of the Word of God personified in Jesus. We are to defend ourselves against the evil one by speaking aloud God's truth.

Why is it so important to speak God's Word in addition to believing it and thinking it? Because Satan is a created being, and he doesn't perfectly know what you're thinking. By observing you he can pretty well tell what you are thinking, just as any student of human behavior can. But he doesn't know what you're going to do before you do it. He can put thoughts into your mind, and he will know whether you buy his lie by how you behave.

In this book I am attempting to influence your mind through the words in this book. But I can't read your thoughts. Similarly, Satan can try to influence you by planting thoughts in your head, but he can't read your thoughts. If you're going to resist Satan, you must do so outwardly so he can understand you and be put to flight.

The two most common misconceptions about Satan are that he can read your mind and that he knows the future. Every occultic practice claims to know the mind (or influence it) or predict the future. But only God knows the thoughts and intents of your mind, and only He knows the future. Never ascribe the divine attributes of God to Satan.

You can communicate with God in your mind and spirit because He knows the thoughts and intents of your heart (Hebrews 4:12). Your unspoken communion with God is your private sanctuary; Satan cannot eavesdrop on you. But by the same token, if you only tell Satan to leave with your thoughts, he won't leave because he can't hear you. *You must defeat Satan by speaking out.* The good news is that most attacks occur at night or when you are alone, so resisting Satan aloud seldom results in you having to explain to other people a vocal command instructing Satan to leave. However, there may be times when you will need to take a public stand against the enemy, which may include confessing with your mouth that Jesus is Lord (Romans 10:9).

Fear has never been a major issue in my life, but one night I woke up absolutely terrified for no apparent reason. It was a fear that made my skin crawl, and I knew it was an attack from Satan. Without lifting my head from the pillow, I applied the two-step remedy suggested by James: "Submit therefore to God. Resist the devil and he will flee from you" (4:7). In the sanctuary of my heart, out of Satan's earshot, I submitted to God by praying, "Lord, I acknowledge Your sovereign grace over my life right now. You are my God." Then I resisted Satan with one spoken word—Jesus—and the fear was instantly and totally gone. I went back to sleep in complete peace.

On another occasion I was preparing to speak in chapel on the topic of deliverance and evangelism, in which I would expose some of the strategies of Satan in these areas. Early that morning I rose and showered before my wife or children were awake. When I stepped out of the shower I found several strange symbols traced on the fogged-up mirror. I didn't do it, and Joanne, Heidi, and Karl were still asleep; they hadn't done it either. I wiped the markings off the mirror, suspicious that someone was flinging darts at me to dissuade me from my chapel message.

I went down to eat breakfast alone, and as I was sitting in the kitchen, suddenly I felt a slight pain on my hand that made me flinch. I looked down to see what appeared to be two little bite-marks on my hand. "Is that your best shot?" I said aloud to the powers of darkness attacking me. "Do you think symbols on the mirror and a little bite are going to keep me from giving my message in chapel today? Get out of here." The nuisance left, and my message in chapel went off without a hitch.

Physical strength has nothing to do with success in spiritual warfare (2 Corinthians 10:4); it is the Lord's strength which sends evil spirits running for cover. The power is in the spoken Word.

THE PROTECTIVE POWER OF PRAYER

The mother of one of my seminary students was a psychic. She said to him once, "Jim, have you been praying for me?"

"Of course I have, Mother."

"Well, don't," she insisted, "because you're disturbing my aura."

I say pray on! We never know completely the effects of our prayers, but we do know that God includes our prayer as part of His strategy for establishing His kingdom.

One of the most dramatic deliverances I have observed happened in a man who was a high priest in the upper echelons of Satanism. Six months after he was set free he gave his testimony in our church. At the close of his testimony I asked him, "Based on your experience on 'the other side,' what is the Christian's first line of defense against demonic influence?"

"Prayer," he answered forcefully. "And when you pray, mean it. Fervent prayer thwarts Satan's activity like nothing else."

What is prayer? It is communication with God by which we express our dependence on Him. God knows what we need in our battle with the powers of darkness, and He is more ready to meet our needs than we are to ask. But until we express our dependence on Him in prayer, God will not act. In prayer we say, "You are the Lord, not I. You know what's best; I don't. I'm not telling you what to do; I'm asking. I declare my dependence on You." Our prayers open the way for God to act on our behalf.

After instructing us to put on the armor that God has provided, Paul wrote: "With all prayer and petition, pray at all times in the Spirit, and with this in view, be on the alert with all perseverance and petition for all the saints" (Ephesians 6:18). I don't have all the answers on what Paul meant by praying in the Spirit, but I do know that praying in the Spirit is God's way of helping us pray when we don't know how to pray: "The Spirit also helps our weakness; for we do not know how to pray as we should, but the Spirit Himself intercedes for us" (Romans 8:26). "Helps" (*sunantilambano*) in this verse beautifully describes how the Holy Spirit comes near to pick us up and carry us safely to the other side. Prayer in the Spirit helps us span chasms of need that we don't know how to cross.

Praying for Spiritual Sight

There are several specific needs which we should consider as targets for prayer in spiritual warfare. One need relates to the condition of blindness which Satan has inflicted on unbelievers (2 Corinthians 4:3,4). People cannot come to Christ unless their spiritual eyes are opened. Theodore Epp wrote, "If Satan has blinded and bound men and women, how can we ever see souls saved? This is where you and I enter the picture. Spoiling the goods of the strong man has to do with liberating those whom Satan has blinded and is keeping bound.... This is where prayer comes in."[2]

Prayer is a primary weapon in combating spiritual blindness. The apostle John wrote: "If we ask anything according to His will, He hears us. And if we know that He hears us in whatever we ask, we know that we have the requests which we have asked from Him" (1 John 5:14,15). Then he immediately challenged believers to apply this principle by asking God to bring life to unbelievers (verse 16). Our evangelistic strategy must include authoritative prayer that God's light would penetrate satanic blindness.

We also need to pray, as Paul did in Ephesians 1:18,19, that the eyes of believers may be enlightened to understand the spiritual power, authority, and protection which is our inheritance in Christ. As long as Satan can keep us in the dark about our position and authority in Christ, he can keep us stunted in our growth and ineffectual in our witness and ministry. We need to pray for each other continually that Satan's smokescreen of lies will be blown away and that our vision into the spiritual realm will be crystal-clear.

Binding the Strong Man

Another target for authoritative prayer is the "strong man" mentioned in Matthew 12:29. Jesus said, referring to Satan and his demons: "How can anyone enter the strong man's house and carry off his property, unless he first binds the strong man?" He was saying that you cannot rescue people from the bonds of spiritual blindness or demonic influence unless you first overpower their captors. Satan's power is already broken, but he will not let go of anything he thinks he can keep until we exercise the authority delegated to us by the Lord Jesus Christ.

When we pray we are not trying to persuade God to join us in *our* service for Him; prayer is the activity of joining God in *His* ministry. By faith we lay hold of the property in Satan's clutches which rightfully belongs to God, and we hold on until Satan turns loose. He will hold on to these people until we demand their release on the basis of our authority in Christ. Once Satan is bound through prayer, he must let go.

In his book *Demon Possession and the Christian*, C. Fred Dickason gives several helpful suggestions for how to pray for someone who is being harassed by demons:

1. Pray that the demons may be cut off from all communication and help from other demons and Satan.

2. Pray that the demons would be confused and weakened in their hold on the person.

3. Pray that the person would be strengthened in his faith to understand his position in Christ and to trust and obey God's Word.

4. Pray that the person may be able to distinguish between his thoughts and feelings and those of Satan.

5. Pray that the person might recognize the demonic presence and not be confused, but willingly seek godly counsel and help.

6. Pray that God would protect and guide His child and set angelic forces at work to break up every scheme of the enemy.[3]

Several years ago a personal experience emphasized to me the power of prayer in dealing with people who are in the clutches of the strong man. I was on the staff of a large church at the time. I came back from lunch one day to find several of our secretaries and custodians drinking coffee and chatting in the lounge near the church office. At the other end of the room was a tall man in his mid-twenties, a total stranger to me, standing at the chalkboard writing tiny words and then erasing them. "Who's that?" I asked my co-workers.

"We don't know. He just walked in."

Amazed that someone hadn't already greeted the man, I walked over and said, "Hi, my name is Neil. Can I help you?"

"Oh, I don't know," he answered rather distantly as he put down the chalk. He looked and sounded like his mind had been blown on drugs, so I decided to get him out of the church and just talk to him for awhile. I discovered that his name was Bill and that he worked at a local car wash. I invited him to come to church. After an hour of conversation he left.

A couple of days later Bill came back and we talked some more. Then about two weeks later on a Sunday afternoon I was in my office getting ready for the evening service when my intercom buzzed. "There's a guy down here named Bill who wants to see you."

"Send him up," I answered.

I really didn't have time for idle chatter, but I was concerned about Bill. "I'm glad you're here, Bill," I began. "May I ask you a personal question?" Bill nodded. "Have you ever trusted in Christ to be your Lord and your Savior?"

"No."

"Would you like to?"

"I don't know, Neil," Bill answered with a slightly troubled expression.

I brought out a salvation tract and read through it with him. "Do you understand this, Bill?"

"Yes."

"Would you like to make that decision for Christ now?"

"Yes."

"I'll pray a simple prayer of commitment, and you repeat it after me phrase by phrase, okay?"

"Okay."

"Lord Jesus, I need you," I began.

Bill began to respond, "Lor-r-r..." Then he locked up completely. I realized that I had invaded the domain of demonic powers, and they didn't want to let go of Bill.

"Bill, there's a battle going on for your mind," I said finally. "I'm going to read some Scripture, and I'm going to pray out loud for you. I'm going to bind the enemy and stand against him. As soon as you can, you just tell Jesus what you believe." His eyes confirmed that the battle was raging.

I started reading Scripture and praying aloud every prayer I could think of to bind Satan and set Bill free. I was still very new at dealing with demonic powers at the time, so I was kind of grasping at straws.

After about 15 minutes of prayer and Scripture Bill suddenly groaned, "Lord Jesus, I need you." Then he slumped back in his chair like he had just gone ten rounds with the world heavyweight champion. He looked at me with tear-filled eyes and said, "I'm free." I had never used the word "freedom" with him; that was his expression. But he was free and he knew it.

Understanding the spiritual nature of our world should have a profound effect on your evangelistic strategy. All too often we proclaim the virtues of Christianity to unbelievers like someone standing outside a prison compound proclaiming to the inmates the virtues of the outside world. But unless someone overpowers the prison guards and opens the gates, how can the prisoners experience the freedom we're telling them about? We must learn to bind the strong man before we will be able to rescue his prisoners.

God has not only equipped you with everything you need to ward off the attack of the strong man, but He has also equipped you and authorized you for search and rescue in the lives of those who are in the devil's clutches. Stand firm in the armor that God has provided and step out in Christ's authority to plunder the strong man's house for God.

PART TWO

Stand Firm!

6

Dealing with Evil in Person

"What in the world happened to Harry?" The woman speaking to me over the phone was referring to her former boyfriend, the satanic high priest I mentioned in the last chapter who found Christ and was set free from unbelievable bondage to darkness. Evelyn told me that she had urged Harry to get out of Satanism, but never expected the transformation which had occurred in him. She wanted some answers.

"I'll be happy to sit down with you and talk about it," I replied. So we set up an appointment at my office.

When Evelyn walked in, all kinds of warning buzzers sounded inside me. Not only did she bring with her a history of intimacy with a high priest in Satanism, but she was also very seductively dressed. I decided to keep my distance and proceed with caution.

As she began to tell me about herself, Evelyn mentioned that she was a Christian, but I had my doubts. I casually inserted into the conversation a couple questions about Evelyn's eternal destiny. True to my suspicions, her answers were filled with self-righteous platitudes. I realized that I was dealing with a very deceived person.

"When Harry and I got together," she continued, "we would go into a Catholic church and she would speak to him there."

"You mean a nun would come and counsel Harry?" I asked.

"No, she would speak to him through me."

Suddenly the light came on. "You're saying that someone inside you was communicating with Harry using your voice, and that this person was a she."

Evelyn nodded. "Not only was she a she, she was Irish."

"Evelyn, the Bible tells us to test the spirits. Did you ever test this spirit?"

"No, I had no reason to."

"Would you be willing to test this spirit now?"

"Sure."

There was a time in my ministry when at this point in the conversation I would have entered into a dialogue with this demon, commanding it to speak to me through Evelyn. But often this kind of approach leads to a power struggle which bypasses the individual. Some people even blank out while I'm wrestling with the spirit and don't remember what happened to them. I have learned that what the *individual* does during a confrontation like this is more important than what *I* do. He or she must take responsibility for renouncing and resisting Satan, and he must personally embrace the truth of Christ. I wanted Evelyn to be fully aware of what was happening to her.

"In the name of Jesus Christ," I prayed, "I bind you to silence, spirit, unless I command you to speak. Now in Christ's name, identify yourself to Evelyn's mind." I wanted Evelyn to tell me what she heard.

A puzzled look came over Evelyn's face. "She says she is Maggie McKendall." What followed was a three-way conversation.

I addressed my questions to the spirit in Evelyn which I had bound to silence on the basis of our authority in Christ. The spirit answered my question by speaking to Evelyn's mind, which she heard as clearly in her head as she heard me with her ears. Then Evelyn, fully awake and participative, verbalized the answer she heard.

"How old are you, Maggie McKendall?" I asked.

"Soul life has no age."

"Why did you come?"

"To help the saints in warfare."

"Were you ever alive on planet Earth?"

"Yes."

"When did you die?"

Evelyn relayed the answer that Maggie McKendall died in the 1970's in Ireland.

If you know your Bible, you know that I wasn't in dialogue with a dead Irish Christian named Maggie McKendall who had returned in spirit form to help the saints in warfare. Jesus' account of the rich man and Lazarus in Luke 16:19-31 clearly reveals that there is a great, impassable chasm between the living and the dead. No one who crosses from life to death can return.

Furthermore, Isaiah commanded God's people: "When they say to you, 'Consult the mediums and the wizards who whisper and mutter,' should not a people consult their God? Should they consult the dead on behalf of the living? To the law and to the testimony! If they do not speak according to this word, it is because they have no dawn" (Isaiah 8:19,20). The only Spirit God has ordained to equip us for warfare is the Holy Spirit.

By that time in the dialogue I was sure that I was dealing with a demon who was deceiving Evelyn into believing that it was there to help her. So I continued with a question which I knew would expose the spirit: "Maggie McKendall, is Jesus your Lord?"

"Yes," Evelyn answered for the spirit.

I was really puzzled. Here was a spirit obviously from the kingdom of darkness who was confessing Jesus Christ as its Lord! I have asked numerous other spirits that question. Some of them respond angrily, "No!" Others of them answer, "Yes, Jesus Christ is *the* Lord." But when I press them by asking if Jesus Christ is *their own* Lord, none of them answer in the affirmative. Either Evelyn wasn't telling me the truth about what she was hearing or else something was very wrong.

"Did Jesus Christ come in the flesh?" I continued.

Again her answer took me off-guard: "Yes."

I was at my wit's end. Not only was I alone in the building with a strange, sensual-looking young woman, but I was totally baffled that the spirit which controlled her claimed Jesus Christ as Lord. I concluded the session rather abruptly and she left.

While I was on my way home it suddenly hit me: I had been deceived too! I hadn't been addressing the spirit; I had been addressing the role which the spirit was playing—that of Maggie McKendall. There likely was an Irish Christian named Maggie McKendall who had died in the 1970's, and the demon in Evelyn was playing that role. As long as I kept questioning Maggie McKendall, the demon was free to answer the way Maggie McKendall would answer: "Yes, Jesus Christ is my Lord." Now when I encounter a spirit who is trying to impersonate someone from the past, I simply say, "That's a lie; you're an evil spirit." Then, if the person is willing, I lead him or her through the steps to freedom. I have also learned how to avoid talking with evil spirits completely and not to believe anything they say. Jesus warned us in John 8:44: "Whenever he [the devil] speaks a lie, he speaks from his own nature; for he is a liar, and the father of lies."

A Rebel Authority Is in Control

My experience with Harry, Evelyn, and "Maggie McKendall"—and countless other expressions of demonic influence and control—illustrate that we live in a world which is under the authority of an evil ruler. Originally God created Adam and his race to rule over creation. But Adam forfeited his position of authority through sin, and Satan became the rebel holder of authority to whom Jesus referred as "the ruler of this world" (John 12:31; 14:30; 16:11). During Jesus' temptation, the devil offered Him "all the kingdoms of the world, and their glory" (Matthew 4:8) in exchange for His worship. Satan's claim that the earth "has been handed over to me, and I give it to whomever I wish" (Luke 4:6) was no lie. He took authority when Adam abdicated the throne of rulership over God's creation at the fall. Satan ruled from Adam until the cross. The death, resurrection, and ascension of Christ secured forever the final authority for Jesus Himself (Matthew 28:18). That authority was extended to all believers in the Great Commission so that we may continue His work of destroying the works of the devil (1 John 3:8).

All of us were born spiritually dead and subject to the ruler that Paul called "the prince of the power of the air" (Ephesians 2:2). But when we received Christ, God "delivered us from the domain of darkness, and transferred us to the kingdom of His beloved Son" (Colossians 1:13). Our citizenship was changed from earth to heaven (Philippians 3:20). Satan is the ruler of this world, but he is no longer *our* ruler, for Christ is our ruler.

But as long as we live on the earth, we are still on Satan's turf. He will try to rule our lives by deceiving us into believing that we still belong to him. As aliens in a foreign, hostile kingdom, we need protection from this evil, deceptive, hurtful tyrant. Christ has not only provided protection from and authority over Satan, but He has equipped us with the Spirit of truth, the indwelling Holy Spirit, to guide us into all truth and help us discern the evil one's schemes (John 16:13).

Even though our eternal destiny is secure and the armor of God is readily available, we are still vulnerable to Satan's accusations, temptations, and deceptions. If we give in to these, we can be influenced by Satan's wishes (Galatians 5:1). And if we remain under his influence long enough, we can lose control. Yes, believers can be controlled by Satan if they fail to stand against him. *Ownership* is never at stake, however. We belong to God, and Satan can't touch our basic identity in Him. But as long as we are living in this body, we can allow ourselves to be vulnerable targets to all his fiery darts.

The Powers That Be

Virtually all evangelical Christians and even many liberals agree that Satan is a living being who is responsible for the evil in the world today. Many confessions of faith used to include a section about believing in a personal devil—not that every person has his own personal devil, but that the devil is an actual personage rather than merely an impersonal force. But when you start talking about demons being alive and active in the world today, a lot of Christians bristle, "Hold on there. I believe in the devil, but I don't buy that stuff about demons."

My question to these people is: How do you think Satan carries on his worldwide ministry of evil and deception? He is a created being. He is not omnipresent, omniscient, or omnipotent. He can't be everywhere in the world tempting and deceiving millions of people at the same moment. He does so through an army of emissaries (demons, evil spirits, fallen angels, etc.) who propogate his plan of rebellion around the world.

Disbelief in personal demonic activity (or an inordinate fear of demons) is further evidences of the static that Satan perpetrates in our minds to distort the truth. In the classic *Screwtape Letters*, C.S. Lewis wrote: "There are two equal and opposite errors into which our race can fall about the devils. One is to disbelieve their existence. The other is to believe and feel an unhealthy interest in them. They themselves are equally pleased by both errors and hail a materialist or a magician with the same delight."[1]

Perhaps the best description of the spiritual host which harasses God's people is found in Ephesians 6:12: "Our struggle is not against flesh and blood, but against the rulers, against the powers, against the world forces of this darkness, against the spiritual forces of wickedness in the heavenly places." Some Christians wonder if the rulers and powers mentioned in this verse refer to ungodly human structures of authority instead of a hierarchy of demons under Satan's headship. Some references to rulers and powers in Scripture specifically designate human authorities (Luke 12:11; Acts 4:26). At other times these terms are used in reference to superhuman powers (Colossians 1:16; 2:15; Romans 8:38,39). It is clear from the context of Ephesians 6:12 that the rulers, powers, and forces which oppose us are spiritual entities in the heavenlies (the spiritual world).

After I led Harry, the former high priest of Satanism, to Christ, I began to learn from talking with him more about the extent and organization of Satanism. He told me that he was not a priest in a local coven, but a member of the council of 50 in a worldwide coven. He shared with me that the organizational structure in Satanism corresponds to the four-level hierarchy of demonic rule under Satan mentioned in Ephesians 6:12. "Rulers" is linked to the royal court of Satanism. There are seven major covens in the world which are presented on the royal court. "Powers" corresponds to host-level priests, and "world forces" to legion-level priests. "Spiritual forces" identifies the circle covens or local covens.

The Satanist organization is massive and extremely secretive. When you hear of satanic priests or rituals, you are hearing only about activities at the level of the circle coven. However, you need not concern yourself too much with what you see or hear, since the Satanist activity which you read about in the newspapers or which is recorded in most police reports is usually the activity of mere dabblers. It's what you *don't* see that is pulling the strings and arranging events in Satanism. I have counseled enough victims of Satanism to know that there are breeders (producing children expressly for sacrifice or for development into leaders) and infiltrators committed to infiltrating and disrupting Christian ministry.

To illustrate how human and spiritual forces of wickedness work together, ask any group of committed Christians this question: "How many of you have been awakened for no apparent reason at 3:00 A.M.?" I ask that question regularly in my conferences, and about two-thirds of the participants raise their hands. Satanists meet from 12:00 to 3:00 A.M., and part of their ritual is to summon and send demons. Three in the morning is prime time for demon activity, and if you have awakened at that time it may be that you have been targeted. I have been targeted by demons numerous times. However, it's not a frightening experience for me, and it shouldn't be for you. John promised, "Greater is He who is in you than he who is in the world" (1 John 4:4). You have authority over Satan's activity and you have the armor of God to protect you. Whenever Satan attacks, you must "be strong in the Lord, and in the strength of His might" (Ephesians 6:10). Consciously place yourself in the Lord's hands, resist Satan with the spoken Word, and go back to sleep. You are only vulnerable when you are walking by sight instead of by faith or walking in the flesh instead of in the Spirit.

What should we do about Satan's hierarchy of demonic powers? Nothing! We are not to be demon-centered; we are to be God-centered and ministry-centered. We are to fix our eyes on Jesus, preach the gospel, love one another, and be God's ambassadors in our fallen world.

THE PERSONALITY OF DEMONS

The Bible does not attempt to prove the existence of demons any more than it attempts to prove the existence of God. It simply reports on their activities as if its first readers accepted their existence. Nor did the early church fathers have a problem with the reality and personality of demons. Origen wrote: "In regard to the devil and his angels and opposing powers, the ecclesiastical teaching maintains that the beings do indeed exist; but what they are or how they exist is not explained with sufficient clarity. This opinion, however, is held by most: that the devil was an angel; and having apostatized, he persuaded as many angels as possible to fall away with himself; and these, even to the present time, are called his angels."[2]

Luke 11:24-26 gives us a helpful view into the personality and individuality of evil spirits. After Jesus cast out a demon which had rendered a man dumb, His detractors accused Him of casting out demons by the power of "Beelzebul, the ruler of the demons" (Luke 11:15). During the discussion of demons which followed, Jesus said: "When the unclean spirit goes out of a man, it passes through waterless places seeking rest, and not finding any, it says, 'I will return to my house from which I came.' And when it comes, it finds it swept and put in order. Then it goes and takes along seven other spirits more evil than itself, and they go in and live there; and the last state of that man becomes worse than the first" (verses 24-26).

We can glean several points of information about evil spirits from this passage.

1. *Demons can exist outside or inside humans.* Demons seem to be spirits which find a measure of rest in organic beings, preferring even swine over nothingness (Mark 5:12). These spirits may take territorial rights and associate with certain geographical locations which have been used for satanic purposes.

2. *They are able to travel at will.* Being spiritual entities, demons are not subject to the barriers of the natural world. The walls of your church building do not establish it as a sanctuary from demonic influence; only prayer and spiritual authority can do that.

3. *They are able to communicate.* It is obvious from Luke 11 that evil spirits can communicate with each other. They can also speak to humans through a human subject, such as they did through the Gadarene demoniac (Matthew 8:28-34). Such extreme cases reveal a takeover of the central nervous system. A lesser degree of control includes

those who pay attention to deceiving spirits (1 Timothy 4:1).

4. *Each one has a separate identity.* Notice the use of personal pronouns in Luke 11: "I will return to my house from which I came" (verse 24). We are dealing with thinking personalities as opposed to an impersonal force. That's why secular methods of research are not going to reveal their existence. Revelation alone is our authoritative source on the reality and personality of evil spirits.

5. *They are able to remember and makes plans.* The fact that they can leave a place, come back, remember their former state, and plan reentry with others shows their ability to think and plan. The concept of "familiar spirits" is well-documented in church history.

6. *They are able to evaluate and make decisions.* The fact that the evil spirit found his human target "swept and put in order" (verse 25) clearly indicates that it can evaluate its intended victim. Demons gain access to our lives through our points of vulnerability. Yet we are not to care what Satan thinks of us; we are to live our lives in a way that is pleasing to God (2 Corinthians 5:9).

7. *They are able to combine forces.* In Luke 11 the one spirit joined with a group of seven others, making the victim's last state worse than his first. In the case of the Gadarene demoniac, the number of demons united for evil was "legion" (Mark 5:9). I have heard many people identify a number of different voices in their mind, describing them as a committee.

8. *They vary in degrees of wickedness.* The first demon in Luke 11 brought back seven other spirits "more evil than itself" (verse 26). Jesus indicated a difference in the wickedness of spirits when He said of one, "This kind cannot come

out by anything but prayer" (Mark 9:29). The concept of variations in power and wickedness fits the hierarchy which Paul lists in Ephesians 6:12. I can personally attest that some cases of dealing with demonized individuals are more difficult than others.

But you need not fear Satan and his demons as long as you cling to God's truth. His only weapon is deception. Irenaeus wrote, "The devil . . . can only go to this length, as he did at the beginning, to deceive and lead astray the mind of man into disobeying the commandments of God, and gradually to darken the hearts."[3] If you continue to walk in the light you don't need to be afraid of the darkness.

Running the Gauntlet of Evil

How do these evil spirits interfere with our lives? Let me answer with a simple illustration. Imagine that you are standing at one end of a long, narrow street lined on both sides with two-story row houses. At the other end of the street stands Jesus Christ, and your Christian life is the process of walking down that long street of maturity in Him. There is absolutely nothing in the street which can keep you from reaching Jesus. So, when you receive Christ, you fix your eyes on Him and start walking.

But since this world is still under the dominion of Satan, the row houses on either side of you are inhabited by beings who are committed to keeping you from reaching your goal. They have no power or authority to block your path or even slow your step, so they hang out of the windows and call to you, hoping to turn your attention away from your goal and disrupt your progress.

One of the ways they will try to distract you is by calling out, "Hey, look over here! I've got something you really want. It tastes good, feels good, and is a lot more fun than your boring walk down the street. Come on in and take a look." That's temptation, suggesting to your mind ways to serve yourself instead of God. We will discuss temptation in greater detail in Chapter 8.

As you continue your walk toward Christ you will also have thoughts like "I'm stupid. I'm ugly. I'll never amount to anything for God." Satan's emissaries are masters at accusation, especially after they have distracted you through temptation. One minute they're saying, "Try this; there's nothing wrong with it." Then, when you yield, they're right there taunting, "See what you did! How can you call yourself a Christian when you behave like that?" Accusation is one of Satan's primary weapons in his attempt to distract you from your goal. We will consider his ploy of accusation more fully in Chapter 9.

Other remarks which are hurled at you as you walk down the street sound like this: "You don't need to go to church today. It's not important to pray and read the Bible every day. Some of the New Age stuff isn't so bad." That's deception, and it is Satan's most subtle and debilitating weapon. You will often hear these messages in first-person singular: "I don't need to go to church today, pray, read my Bible," etc. Satan knows you will be more easily deceived if he can make you think the thought was yours instead of his. Satan's strategy of deception will be more fully explored in Chapter 10.

What is the enemy's goal in having his demons jeer you, taunt you, lure you, and question you from the windows and doorways along your path? He wants you to slow down, stop, sit down, and if possible, give up your journey toward Christ. He wants to influence you to doubt your ability to believe and serve God. Remember: He has absolutely no power or authority to keep you from steadily progressing in your walk toward Christ. And he can never again own you, because you have been redeemed by Jesus Christ and you are forever in Him (1 Peter 1:18,19). But if he can get you to listen to the thoughts he plants in your mind, he can influence you. And if you allow him to influence you long enough through temptation, accusation, and deception, he can control you. We'll talk more about the extent of demonic control in a Christian's life in Chapter 11.

Levels of Bondage

There are several levels of spiritual freedom and bondage between the apostle Paul, whose Christian life and ministry were exemplary despite his battle with sin and Satan (Romans 7:15-25; 2 Corinthians 12:7-9), and the Gadarene demoniac, who was totally controlled by demons (Matthew 8:28-34). Nobody loses control to Satan overnight; it's a gradual process of deception and yielding to his subtle influence. It is my observation that no more than 15 percent of the evangelical Christian community is completely free of Satan's bondage. These are the people who are consistently living a Spirit-filled life and bearing fruit. The other 85 percent are struggling along fruitlessly at one of at least three levels of spiritual conflict.

First, a believer may lead a fairly normal Christian life on the outside while wrestling with a steady barrage of sinful thoughts on the inside: lust, envy, greed, hatred, apathy, etc. This person has virtually no devotional life. Prayer is a frustrating experience for him, and he usually struggles with interpersonal relationships. Most Christians in this condition have no idea that they are in the middle of a spiritual conflict. They would not identify with the concept of hearing voices, but would readily admit to a problem-filled thought life.

Instead of recognizing that their minds are being peppered by the fiery darts of the enemy, they think the problem is their own fault. "If those foul thoughts are mine, what kind of person am I?" they wonder. So they end up condemning themselves while the enemy continues his attack unchecked. I see about 65 percent of all Christians living at this level of spiritual conflict.

The second level of conflict is characterized by those who can distinguish between their own thoughts and strange, evil "voices" which seem to overpower them. "What am I thinking?" they wonder with alarm when a barrage of sinful ideas, thoughts, and fantasies floods their minds. They experience no victory and wonder if they are cracking up, but they are so frightened by the prospect that they won't share it with anyone. Yet the majority of Christians at this stage still fail to see their struggle as a spiritual conflict. They seek counseling and try to discipline their thoughts, but they experience little or no improvement. I estimate that about 15 percent of all Christians fall into this category. Most of these people are depressed, anxious, paranoid, bitter, or angry, and they may have fallen victim to drinking, drugs, eating disorders, etc.

At the third level of conflict, the individual has lost control and hears voices inside his mind which tell him what to think, say, and do. These people stay at home, wander the streets talking to imaginary people, or occupy beds in mental institutions or rehab units. Sadly, about 5 percent of the Christian community falls victim to this level of deception and control.

When an individual gives in to the inner voices long enough, he is subject to severe oppression by demonic powers, as exemplified in the Gadarene demoniac. The evil spirits exert such control that the individual's personality can be largely bypassed for long periods of time.

Just Say No

There are three ways of responding to the demonic taunts and barbs being thrown at you from those second-story windows during your daily walk with Christ, and two of these ways are wrong.

First, the most defeated people are those who consider demonic thoughts and believe them. A subtle thought is shot into your mind: "You don't pray, read your Bible, or witness like you should. How could God love you?" That's a bald-faced lie, because God's love is unconditional. But you start thinking about your failures and agreeing that you're probably not very lovable to God. Pretty soon you're sitting in the middle of the street going nowhere.

These Christians are totally defeated simply because they have been duped into believing that God doesn't love them, or that they will never be a victorious Christian, or that they are a helpless victim of the past. There is no reason why they can't get up immediately and start walking again, but they have believed a lie and they can't go anywhere.

The second response is just as unproductive. You try to argue with the demons: "I am not ugly or stupid. I am a victorious Christian." You're proud that you don't believe what they say, but they're still controlling you and setting your agenda. You're standing in the middle of the street shouting at them when you should be marching forward.

We are not to believe evil spirits, nor are we to dialogue with them. Instead, we are to ignore them. You're equipped with the armor of God; they can't touch you unless you drop your guard. With every arrow of temptation, accusation, or deception they shoot at you, simply raise the shield of faith, deflect the attack, and walk on (Colossians 2:6). Take every thought captive to the obedience of Christ. Choose truth in the face of every lie. As you do, you will find your maturity and freedom increasing with every step.

7

The Lure of Knowledge and Power

In previous chapters I alluded to Harry, the former high priest of Satanism whose conversion shook up his girlfriend Evelyn. Now I want to tell you Harry's story to illustrate a point of vulnerability we share with him.

Even though Evelyn wasn't a Christian, something about her caused Harry to wonder if there was more to life than he had experienced during his first 45 years. To the casual observer, Harry was a normal Southern California businessman who dabbled in psychic phenomena. At one time he was the president of a large local psychic research society. But his psychic interests were little more than a hobby, a guise to cover his Satanist activities. His mother had been a high priestess in Satanism and had groomed him for his secretive role in Satan worship. He was involved in hard-core Satanism at a level that very few people ever hear about.

Six months before he came to see me, Harry had decided to walk away from Satanism. But when he tried, the powers of darkness held onto their prize in a frightful way, resulting in violent physical outbursts. His landlady, a backslidden Christian and former girlfriend, was deeply frightened, so she called the paramedics. The demonic influence held Harry in such bondage that it took seven paramedics to restrain him.

It is important to understand that demonic influence is not an external force in the physical realm; it is the internal manipulation of the central nervous system. The physical power that a demoniac possesses is similar to the extraordinary adrenaline-driven power exerted in a crisis that allows a mother to lift a car which has overturned on her child in an accident.

After observing Harry for a day, the doctors couldn't find anything wrong with him and let him go. After several futile attempts at helping Harry get out of Satanism, Evelyn was referred to me. She called and set up an appointment for him.

Harry came to my office of his own accord, but he was uneasy about the battle which he anticipated. Once he was seated he said, "You have no idea what kind of power you're up against."

"Yes, I think I *do* understand the power of Satan," I answered calmly. "But you obviously have no idea of the power of God. You say you want to get out of the darkness, but you have discovered that you can't do it on your own. In order to be free you must choose Christ as your Lord; only He can set you free. Are you prepared to choose Christ?"

Harry began to shake a little, and I realized that the enemy wasn't going to give up without a fight. I decided that I needed some additional support for prayer and accountability, so I left Harry in my office while I went to look for someone who could join me. The only person I could find was Wayne, our custodian. Wayne agreed to sit in my office and pray as I dealt with Harry. Wayne was a good Christian man who had served as an elder in our church. But I knew he had never seen anything like what he was about to see!

I sat down facing Harry and said, "Are you prepared to make a decision for Christ, Harry?" He started to fidget a little in his chair. When he tried to answer me, suddenly it was showtime. He exploded with a bloodcurdling roar, then stood up and was seemingly thrown across the room. He ranted and raved and rolled around the office like a crazy man. The demons who controlled Harry were using his mind, his will, his muscles, and his emotions in a noisy display of resistance.

By this time Wayne was plastered against the wall, praying like he had never prayed in his life! But I just sat still. I learned a long time ago that Satan's show of power is just another facet of his deception designed to provoke fear. He knows that if he can deceive us into being afraid of him, fear will control our life instead of faith. Satan "prowls about like a roaring lion, seeking someone to devour" (1 Peter 5:8). Why does a lion roar? To paralyze its prey with fear. Once its victim is immobilized by fear, the lion can easily subdue it and kill it.

But because of our position, authority, and protection in Christ, Satan can't touch us. Fear is a powerful controller, but the only thing we have to fear is fear itself. If you cower in fear at Satan's show of power, then he has you on the defensive. But Peter instructed, "Resist him, firm in your faith" (1 Peter 5:9). Satan is defeated; believe it and stand up to him. When you do, he has no choice but to eventually back down.

As the devil roared at me through Harry, I began to read Scripture aloud and pray in a normal, controlled voice that the enemy would be bound in silence. The portion of Scripture I usually read in these encounters is Ephesians 1, which graphically describes our position and authority in Christ. After I had spent several minutes taking authority in Christ through prayer and reading Scripture, Harry fell flat on his stomach in front of me. "Lord Jesus, I need you!" he cried out. I led him in a prayer of commitment to Christ. And when Harry finally stood up he was free. He embraced Wayne and me with a childlike joy he had never experienced before.

But even though Harry was set free from Satan's control of his life, he had trouble staying free. He was kind of like an alcoholic who comes to Christ. When an alcoholic receives Christ, he is totally alive spiritually. But unless God intervenes in an unusual way, he has to live with the damage he has done to his liver and with the patterns, habits, and cravings which were ingrained in his brain over the years.

Similarly, Harry had been deeply involved in unspeakable satanic rituals for most of his life. Once he made a decision for Christ, he couldn't just walk away from his past as if it had never happened. He continued to battle the physical, mental, and emotional effects of his bondage.

Other Satanists made several attempts on Harry's life and harassed him mentally day and night. They contacted Harry and agreed to stop the demonic mental assault on him if he would sign an agreement not to share his testimony again as he had at our church. Harry signed the agreement, and I haven't heard from him since.

A TRAP AS OLD AS THE BIBLE

How do people like Harry get trapped in the diabolical quagmire of Satan's control in the first place? More important, what are some of the pitfalls we need to avoid which, if we tumble into them, will keep us from experiencing and maintaining the freedom which is ours in Christ?

The lure of the occult is almost always on the basis of acquiring knowledge or power. We crave a knowledge that is esoteric, not normally available to the ordinary person. We want to experience a power that is spiritual and supernatural in origin. In a sense these are God-given desires, but they are intended to be fulfilled by the knowledge and power which comes from *God*. However, Satan is busy trying to pass off his counterfeits for God's knowledge and power as the real thing. If he can get you to accept his versions of knowledge and power, he has a foothold in your life.

The lure of satanic knowledge and power is nothing new. God's people have been warned against it from the earliest times. Moses commanded the people on the eve of their invasion of the Promised Land:

> When you enter the land which the Lord your God gives you, you shall not learn to imitate the detestable

things of those nations. There shall not be found among you anyone who makes his son or his daughter pass through the fire, one who uses divination, one who practices witchcraft, or one who interprets omens, or a sorcerer, or one who casts a spell, or a medium, or a spiritist, or one who calls up the dead. For whoever does these things is detestable to the Lord; and because of these detestable things the Lord your God will drive them out before you. You shall be blameless before the Lord your God (Deuteronomy 18:9-13).

This command is as viable for us today as it was for the Israelites under Moses's leadership. We live in a contemporary Canaan where it is socially acceptable to consult spiritists, mediums, palm-readers, psychic counselors, and horoscopes for special esoteric insights and abilities. This was clearly brought home to me while I was finishing my doctorate in a class I took on futures. One of the men in the class, a school principal from Los Angeles, presented a paper describing a scenario of the future he had researched. He excitedly explained that we were on the threshold of new frontiers in the mind: astral projection, telepathic images, levitation, etc. It was nothing but New Age and the occult, and the other class members—all doctoral candidates in the field of public education—were eating it up.

After the class had enjoyed several minutes of lively discussion I raised my hand and said, "In all your exploration of your subject, did you ever ask yourself if it is right for people to get involved in it?"

"Oh, I'm not interested in whether it's right or not," he replied. "I just know it works."

"I have no question that it works," I argued. "Spiritual phenomena and occultic practices are as old as biblical history. The question we need to answer is not whether or not it works, but whether or not it's right." My comments ended the class, and many turned to question me about why dabbling in the occult is wrong.

I'm also aware that the dark side of Satan's versions of spiritual knowledge and power mentioned by Moses—ritual sacrifice, witchcraft, sorcery—are thriving in our culture, though not as openly. Our police departments are trying to tell parents today, "Wake up! Your kids are not just into drugs and illicit sex. They're into *Satanism.* We've seen the blood and the mutilated animals." It's getting so bad that one of the animal control agencies in our area will no longer release a black dog or cat for fear that it will become the victim of satanic ritual abuse.

The man who heads up our campus security belongs to a group of security officers from campuses across Southern California which meets once a month. When it was our school's turn to host the meeting, he asked me to speak to the group about spiritual phenomena in our culture. "There aren't many Christians in the group," he said, "but they'll be on our campus, so I want you to speak to them." I agreed to do so.

It was a veteran crowd of former military men and police officers. When I started talking about the rise of Satanism and ritual abuse in our community, there wasn't a doubter or a scoffer in the bunch. Every one of them had a story to share about finding grisly evidence of Satanism being active on their respective campuses.

Every aberration of spiritual knowledge and power that Moses warned the Israelites to avoid in Canaan—from "harmless" horoscopes to unthinkable atrocities of animal and human sacrifice—is in place and operating in our culture today. And they all have their root in Satan's deception.

KNOWLEDGE FROM THE DARK SIDE

The craving for esoteric, "extra" knowledge in our culture was starkly illustrated to me when two conferences, both open to the public, were recently held in Pasadena, California. One was a major world conference on international missions, and about 600 people attended. At the same time, a New Age conference was being conducted in the Pasadena Civic Center, and more than 40,000 people showed up! That's our society today. People don't want to hear what God has to say. They want information and direction from someone else who "knows": a psychic, a channeler, a palm-reader, a card-reader, or the spirit of a dead friend or relative.

The Scriptures are very clear on the subject of seeking knowledge and direction for our lives from anyone but God: "Do not turn to mediums or spiritists; do not seek them out to be defiled by them.... As for the person who turns to mediums and to spiritists, to play the harlot after them, I will also set My face against that person and will cut him off from among his people.... A man or a woman who is a medium or a spiritist shall surely be put to death" (Leviticus 19:31; 20:6,27).

We're about as far away from that stance on the purveyors of psychic and spiritual advice as we can be. We have people channeling on TV and radio programs, and they're considered celebrities. I read recently that more women in Los Angeles consult spiritists than professional counselors. You can attend a psychic fair in practically any city in our land and get a personal spiritual "reading." The reader is either a fake or a spiritual medium who enters a trance and seemingly receives instruction for you from the spiritual world. Far from being seen as a blight on society, these people are often revered as highly as doctors and ministers for their "expertise."

Charlatans and Real Mediums

Where do mediums and spiritists get their "amazing" information and insights? Many of them are tied into demonic influences, but much of what is called spiritism and psychic phenomena is no more than clever illusion. These so-called spiritists give what is referred to as "cold readings." You go to them for advice or direction, and they ask you a few simple, leading questions. Based on the information you give they make general observations which are probably true of most people in your situation. But you're so impressed with the accuracy of their "revelations" that you start tipping them off to all kinds of details which they can fabricate into their "reading." This is not demonic; it's just mental and verbal sleight-of-hand.

But the mediums and spiritists that God warned against in Leviticus and Deuteronomy were not con artists, but people who possessed and passed on knowledge which didn't come through natural channels of perception. These people have opened themselves up to the spirit world and become channels of knowledge from Satan. The charlatan with his phony cold readings is only interested in bilking you of your money. But the false knowledge and direction which comes from Satan through a medium is intended to bilk you of your spiritual vitality and freedom.

I once counseled the victim of a medium. Rory, a sharp-looking man in his late forties who had just gone through a divorce, came into my office and told me his incredible story. One day he took a new lady friend named Bernice on a date to one of our Southern California theme parks. While they were walking through the shops they came to a little store advertising a resident psychic. The sign read: "Come in and receive instructions for your life."

Rory and Bernice went inside, and the psychic astounded them with her esoteric knowledge. Whether she was a true medium receiving her information from a familiar spirit or a clever con artist, I don't know. But the effect on the couple was profound. "If you have this kind of power," Rory exclaimed, "what else can you do for me?" The psychic promised that she could help him become a success in his job and all other areas of life.

Rory fell for it, and he and Bernice began seeing the psychic regularly. One of the woman's first points of advice was that the couple should marry, which they did. They continued to seek and follow the psychic's advice for their lives.

Almost four years later Rory was in my office. His marriage to Bernice was a disaster, and the job which the woman had promised would be so successful had dissolved. When I asked him how much money he had poured down the drain in his pursuit of "spiritual" knowledge, Rory answered, "I personally gave her almost 15,000 dollars, but Bernice lost over 65,000 dollars."

There's big money in these psychic/con artist operations, and a lot of magicians are raking it in. Many people crave to know something extra about their lives and their future, and they will pay handsomely if they think you can give them the inside information they desire.

The Down Side of Seeking the Dark Side

Not much is known about the biblical terms "medium" and "spiritist." Since "medium" (*ob*, meaning witch, necromancer, or one with a familiar spirit) is feminine, and spiritist (*yidd oni*, from the root "to know") is masculine, some think that they are male and female counterparts of the same role.

The Old Testament abounds with illustrations of kings, false prophets, and mediums leading the nation of Israel in rebellion against God. One of the more well-known cases was Israel's first king. Saul began well by seeking God's guidance and was appointed by Samuel as King of Israel (1 Samuel 9). And he served well until his infamous rebellion against God's will (1 Samuel 15), a sin which God equates with the sin of divination (verse 23). Why did Saul sin and reject the word of the Lord? Because he feared the voice of the people more than the voice of God—a problem all too evident in our world today. The problem of rebellion is the worst problem in the world.

Although Saul was sorry that he sinned (or at least sorry that he was caught!), there is no evidence which suggests that he was truly repentant. Like many people who disobey God, he tried to rectify his mistake, but it was too late and "the Spirit of the Lord departed from Saul, and an evil spirit from the Lord terrorized him" (1 Samuel 16:14).

This is a difficult passage for two reasons. First, it seems to imply that a person can lose the Holy Spirit by an act of disobedience. But it must be understood that the presence of the Holy Spirit in the Old Testament was selective and temporary. The Spirit involved with Saul was probably the same Spirit involved with David in verse 13: a special equipping of the Spirit for ruling as God's anointed king. This unique equipping is not the same as the personal relationship in the Spirit that we enjoy with God as His children today.

Beginning after the cross, the church is identified by the indwelling presence of the Holy Spirit, who forever unites the children of God with their heavenly Father (Ephesians 1:13,14). Jesus promised that no one shall snatch us out of His hand (John 10:28), and Paul assured that nothing—not even disobedience—can separate us from the love of God (Romans 8:35-39). We are secure in Christ and indwelt by His Spirit through faith in the work of Christ on the cross.

The second problem concerns the bothersome idea that an evil spirit could come from the Lord. But we must remember that God is supreme, and He can use Satan and his emissaries as a means to discipline His people as He did with Saul. This is no different from God using a godless nation like Assyria as "the rod of My anger" to discipline His people (Isaiah 10:5,6). It is not inconsistent with the nature or plan of God to use demons to accomplish His will.

Even the church is permitted to turn a grossly immoral member over to Satan "for the destruction of his flesh, that his spirit may be saved in the day of the Lord Jesus" (1 Corinthians 5:5). Why? So the world and its ruler can do a number on such a person in order to prompt genuine repentance. "Do you want to do the devil's bidding?" we ask the immoral believer through this strategy. "Go ahead, and maybe the painful consequences you suffer from your immorality will turn you back to God."

It is interesting to note that whenever the evil spirit came upon Saul, David (the heir apparent to Israel's throne) would play his harp and the evil spirit would depart (1 Samuel 16:23). How pathetically unaware we are of the biblical prominence of music in the spiritual realm! When Elisha was about to inquire of God, he said, " 'Now bring me a minstrel.' And it came about, when the minstrel played, that the hand of the Lord came upon him" (2 Kings 3:15). During the reign of David, over 4000 musicians were assigned to sing in the temple night and day (1 Chronicles 9:33; 23:5). It is the mark of Spirit-filled Christians to sing and make melody in their hearts to the Lord and speak to each other in psalms, hymns, and spiritual songs (Ephesians 5:18-20).

On the other side of the truth lies the destructive power of secular music. Harry, the satanic high priest, showed me numerous symbols on popular record albums indicating commitment and bondage to Satanism. He told me that about 85 percent of today's heavy metal and punk music groups are "owned" by Satanists. They have unwittingly sold themselves to Satanism in exchange for fame and fortune. Few of these artists actually practice Satanism, but most are hopelessly lost and lead others astray through the godless message in their music.

After Samuel the prophet died, Saul's twisted thirst for spiritual knowledge led him to seek guidance from a medium. Having previously purged the nation of mediums and spiritists (1 Samuel 28:3), Saul was directed to the witch of Endor, who had somehow escaped the purge. Coming to the witch in disguise, Saul persuaded her to call up Samuel (verses 8-19). But the scheme backfired when God permitted Samuel himself to return, terrifying the medium (who was expecting a familiar spirit). Samuel's message to Saul was nothing but bad news, foretelling the imminent capture of Israel by the Philistines and the death of Saul and his sons (verse 19).

God expressly forbids necromancy (Isaiah 8:19,20), and the story of the rich man and Lazarus teaches the present-day impossibility of communicating with the dead (Luke 16:19-31). When a psychic claims to have contacted the dead, don't believe it. When a psychologist claims to have regressed a client back to a former existence through hypnosis, don't believe it. When a New Age medium purports to channel a person from the past into the present, realize that it is nothing more than a familiar spirit or the fraudulent work of a con artist.

An Old Idea in New Clothing

The New Age movement cloaks the occult in the description of New Age enlightenment: "You don't need God; you *are* God. You don't need to repent of your sins and depend on God to save you. Sin isn't a problem; you just need to turn off your mind and tune in to the great cosmic oneness through harmonic convergence." The New Age pitch is the oldest lie of Satan: "You will be like God" (Genesis 3:5).

This thirst for knowledge and power has lured a fallen humanity to seek guidance from mediums and spiritists, and from such occultic practices as fortune-telling, tarot cards, palm-reading, Ouija boards, astrology, magic charming, and automatic writing. "Is it because there is no God in Israel that you are going to inquire of Baal-zebub?" Elijah lamented (2 Kings 1:3). People all around us are ignoring the God who loves them and wants to guide their lives, and are instead seeking light and peace in the kingdom of darkness. We may well ask with Jehu, "What peace, so long as the harlotries of your mother Jezebel and her witchcrafts are so many?" (2 Kings 9:22). Peace can only be found in the Prince of Peace, not in the prince of darkness.

Don't be carried away by the prospect of knowledge and power which is luring so many people in our culture today away from God. People such as the devotees of Simon in Acts 8:9,10 will continue to be astonished by those who practice New Age sorcery. Others, such as the customers of the demon-possessed slave girl in Acts 16:16-18 will contribute to the profit of those who exercise a spirit of divination. As in these examples from the early church, those who seek knowledge and power from the dark side will greatly interfere with the work of God, deceiving many by the counterfeit forces they employ. Other people will thirst after power to such an extent that they will sacrifice to the "goat demons" (Leviticus 17:7) and even sacrifice their own children to demons (Psalm 106:36-38). I can verify firsthand from my counseling experience that these kinds of things are actually happening today.

Let these words from Scripture sober us to the reality that even believers are vulnerable to being lured away from the knowledge and power of God by our enemy, who exaggerates our sense of independence and importance apart from God:

> But Jeshurun grew fat and kicked—you are grown fat, thick, and sleek—then he forsook God who made him, and scorned the Rock of his salvation. They made Him jealous with strange gods; with abominations they provoked Him to anger. They sacrificed to demons who were not God, to gods whom they have not known, new gods who came lately, whom your fathers did not dread. You neglected the Rock who begot you, and forgot the God who gave you birth (Deuteronomy 32:15-18).

8

Enticed to Do It Your Way

When our children were young we struggled through the ritual of family devotions. One harried evening we inadvertently overlooked our time of Bible reading and prayer with Heidi and Karl. Several minutes after we had put them to bed we heard Heidi's voice from down the hall: "Daddy, we forgot to do our commotions." "Commotions" were what devotions usually were in our family!

The devotional series I remember best was a continuing discussion with Karl about temptation. For several weeks all he wanted to talk about was temptation. I think he was mainly fascinated by the sound of the word, just like I used to like to say the word "aluminum" when I was a child. But even after several weeks of discussion on the subject, Karl couldn't distinguish the concept of temptation from the act of sin itself.

I have found that many Christian adults struggle with that distinction. Bombarded by tempting thoughts, they conclude that there must be something pretty sick about them. They equate temptation with sin. But even Jesus was "tempted in all things as we are." But finish the verse: "Yet without sin" (Hebrews 4:15). As long as we are in the world we are exposed to temptation just like Jesus was. But He didn't sin, and we don't have to sin either (1 Corinthians 10:13). In this chapter I want to define and describe temptation so you can easily recognize it and quickly refuse Satan's invitation to do things your own way.

THE BASIS OF TEMPTATION

Since Adam, every person is born into this world physically alive and spiritually dead (Ephesians 2:1). Having no relationship with God as we progressed through our developmental years, we learned to live independently of Him, and we attempted to get our needs met apart from Him. We developed patterns of thought and habits of behavior which centered our interests on ourselves.

When we were born again we became spiritually alive, but our flesh, that collection of ingrained, self-centered habits and patterns which we learned when we were spiritually dead, remains to contest our commitment to walk in the Spirit. The essence of temptation is the enticement to have legitimate human needs met through the resources of the world, the flesh, and the devil instead of through Christ (Philippians 4:19). Every temptation is an invitation to live independently of God.

The power of temptation depends on the strength of the strongholds which have been developed in our minds as we learned to live independently of God. For example, if you were raised in a Christian home where dirty magazines and television programs of questionable moral value were not allowed, the power of sexual temptations in your life will not be as great as for someone who grew up exposed to pornographic materials. Why? Because your legitimate need to be loved and accepted was met by caring parents who also protected you from exposure to illegitimate means of establishing your identity and worth. The person who grew up in an environment of immorality and sexual permissiveness will experience a greater struggle with sexual temptation after he becomes a Christian simply because that stronghold was well-established before he was born again.

Too Much of a Good Thing

Most of us won't often be tempted to commit obvious sins such as armed robbery, murder, or rape. Satan is too clever and subtle for that. He knows that we will recognize the flagrant wrong in such temptations and refuse to act on them. Instead, his tack is to entice us to push something good beyond the boundary of the will of God until it becomes sin. He treats us like the proverbial frog in the pot of water: gradually turning up the heat of temptation, hoping we don't notice that we are approaching the boundary of God's will, and jump out before something good becomes sin.

Paul wrote, "All things are lawful for me, but not all things are profitable. All things are lawful for me, but I will not be mastered by anything" (1 Corinthians 6:12). He saw nothing but green lights in every direction of the Christian life. Everything is good and lawful for us because we are free from sin and no longer under the condemnation of the law. But Paul also knew that if we irresponsibly floorboard our lives in any of these good and lawful directions we will eventually run the red light of God's will, and that's sin.

The following statements reveal the sinful results in a number of areas where we are tempted to take the good things that God created beyond the boundary of God's will:

- physical rest becomes laziness
- quietness becomes noncommunication
- ability to profit becomes avarice and greed
- enjoyment of life becomes intemperance
- physical pleasure becomes sensuality
- interest in the possessions of others becomes covetousness
- enjoyment of food becomes gluttony
- self-care becomes selfishness
- self-respect becomes conceit
- communication becomes gossip

- cautiousness becomes unbelief
- positiveness becomes insensitivity
- anger becomes rage and bad temper
- lovingkindness becomes overprotection
- judgment becomes criticism
- same-sex friendship becomes homosexuality
- sexual freedom becomes immorality
- conscientiousness becomes perfectionism
- generosity becomes wastefulness
- self-protection becomes dishonesty
- carefulness becomes fear

Sin Versus Growth

First John 2:12-14 describes three levels of Christian growth in relation to sin. The first level is compared to "little children" (verse 12). Little children in the faith are characterized by having their sins forgiven and possessing a knowledge of God. In other words, they are in the family of God and have overcome the penalty of sin, but they haven't grown to the full maturity.

The second level is "young men" (verses 13,14), those who have overcome the evil one. These are aggressively growing believers who are strong because the Word of God abides in them. They know the truth and how to use it to resist Satan in the battle for their minds. They are no longer in bondage to uncontrollable habits, and they have resolved the personal and spiritual conflicts which keep many Christians from experiencing freedom in Christ. They are free, and they know how to stay free.

The third level is "fathers" (verses 13,14), those who have developed a deep personal knowledge of God. Their faith is securely founded on a close, intimate, loving relationship with God, which is the goal of our spiritual growth. Having challenged us to combat sin's power in our lives through a commitment to growth, John goes on to describe the avenues through which Satan tempts us.

CHANNELS OF TEMPTATION

You will be better prepared to resist temptation in your life when you realize that, according to the Scriptures, there are only three channels through which Satan will entice you to act independently of God. They are summarized in John's instructions to believers concerning our relationship to this world: "Do not love the world, nor the things in the world. If anyone loves the world, the love of the Father is not in him. For all that is in the world, the lust of the flesh and the lust of the eyes and the boastful pride of life, is not from the Father but is from the world. And the world is passing away, and also its lusts; but the one who does the will of God abides forever" (1 John 2:15-17).

The three channels of temptation are the *lust of the flesh*, the *lust of the eyes*, and the *pride of life*. The lust of the flesh preys on our physical appetites and their gratifications in this world. The lust of the eyes appeals to self-interest and tests the Word of God. The pride of life stresses self-promotion and self-exaltation. Satan confronted both the first Adam and the last Adam through each of these three channels of temptation. The first Adam failed miserably, and we still suffer the results of his failure. But the last Adam—Jesus Christ—met Satan's threefold temptation head-on and succeeded triumphantly. In Him we have the resources and the power to conquer every temptation which Satan throws at us. (See Figure 8a on page 130.)

The Lust of the Flesh

Satan first approached Eve through the channel of the lust of the flesh. He planted a doubt in her mind about the

Channel of Temptation (1 Jn. 2:15-17)	Lust of the flesh (animal appetites, cravings, passions) "the woman saw that the tree was good for food..." (Gen. 3:6a).	Lust of the eyes (selfishness, self-interest) "...and that it was a delight to the eyes..." (Gen. 3:6b).	Pride of life (self promotion, self-exaltation) "...and that the tree was desirable to make one wise" (Gen. 3:6c).
Draws us away from the	Will of God (Gal. 5:16f)	Word of God (Mt. 16:24f)	Worship of God (1 Pt. 5:5-11)
Destroys our	Dependence upon God (Jn. 15:5)	Confidence in God (Jn. 15:7)	Obedience to God (Jn. 15:8-10)
First Adam (Gen. 3:1-6)	"Indeed, has God said, 'You shall not eat from any tree of the garden?'"	"You surely shall not die!"	"You will be like God..."
Last Adam (Mt. 4:1-11)	"Man does not live by bread alone, but man lives by everything that proceeds out of the mouth of the Lord" (Dt. 8:3).	"You shall not put the Lord your God to the test" (Dt. 6:16).	"You shall fear only the Lord your God; and you shall worship Him..." (Dt. 6:13).

Figure 8a

fruit of the tree when he said: "Has God said, 'You shall not eat from any tree of the garden'?" (Genesis 3:1). Eve answered, "God has said, 'You shall not eat from it or touch it'" (verse 3). But Satan had piqued her appetite for the forbidden fruit, and she "saw that the tree was good for food" (verse 6). Yielding to the lust of the flesh contributed to Adam and Eve's downfall.

Satan also challenged Jesus through the channel of the lust of the flesh. Our Lord had been fasting for 40 days when Satan tempted Him in the wilderness at the point of His apparent vulnerability: "If You are the Son of God, command that these stones become bread" (Matthew 4:3). Satan is not omniscient, but he's not blind either. He learned about Jesus' apparent vulnerability to physical temptation by watching Him go without food for 40 days. He's watching you too, looking for soft spots of vulnerability in your physical appetites for food, rest, comfort, and sex. Temptation is greatest when hunger, fatigue, and loneliness are acute.

The temptation of the lust of the flesh is designed to draw us away from the will of God to serve the flesh (Galatians 5:16,17). There is nothing sinful about eating per se, and there was nothing intrinsically evil about the forbidden fruit in the Garden of Eden. Eating is a legitimate physical need, and God created food so we could meet that need. But concerning the fruit of one tree God had said, "Don't eat it," and by eating, Adam and Eve violated God's will and acted independently of Him.

Similarly, there was nothing wrong with Jesus eating bread at the end of His fast, except that it wasn't the Father's will for Him to do so. Jesus replied: "Man shall not live on bread alone, but on every word that proceeds out of the mouth of God" (Matthew 4:4). No matter how desirable a loaf of bread may have seemed to Jesus in His state of hunger, He was not about to act independently of the Father's will by accepting Satan's offer. The life that Jesus modeled was a life totally dependent on God the Father (John 5:30; 6:57; 8:42; 14:10; 17:7).

When Satan tempts you through the channel of the lust of the flesh, he will invite you to fulfill your physical needs in ways that are outside the boundary of God's will. Eating is necessary and right, but eating too much, eating the wrong kinds of foods, and allowing food to rule your life are wrong. Sex as intended by God is beautiful and good, but sex outside of marriage, homosexuality, and selfish sex are out-of-bounds and lead to bondage. Whenever you feel enticed to meet a legitimate physical need by acting independently of God, you are being tempted through the lust of the flesh.

When you resist the temptations of the lust of the flesh, you are declaring your dependence on God for your natural needs. As such you are remaining "in the vine," tapping into the resources Jesus referred to in John 15:5. But when you yield to temptation in this area your fruitfulness as a Christian will suffer, because apart from Christ you can do nothing.

The Lust of the Eyes

The second channel of temptation through which Satan came to Adam and Eve related to his lie concerning the consequences of disobeying God. God had said that death would accompany disobedience, but Satan said, "You surely shall not die!" (Genesis 3:4). He was appealing to Eve's sense of self-preservation by falsely assuring her that God was wrong on the issue of sin's consequences. "Don't listen to Him; do what's right in your own eyes," he urged. The forbidden fruit was a delight to her eyes (verse 6), so she and Adam ignored God's command in order to do what appeared to serve their own best interests.

The lust of the eyes subtly draws us away from the Word of God and eats away at our confidence in God. We see what the world has to offer and desire it above our relationship with God. We begin to place more credence in our own perspective of life than in God's commands and promises.

Fueled by the lust for what we see, we grab for all we can get, believing that we need it and deceived that God wants us to have it. Wrongly assuming that God will withhold nothing good from us, we lustfully claim prosperity.

Instead of trusting God wholeheartedly, we adopt a "prove it to me" attitude. That was the essence of Satan's second temptation of Jesus: "If You are the Son of God, throw Yourself down [from the pinnacle of the temple]; for it is written, 'He will give His angels charge concerning You'; and 'On their hands they will bear You up, lest You strike your foot against a stone'" (Matthew 4:6). But Jesus wasn't about to play Satan's "show me" game. He replied, "It is written, 'You shall not put the Lord your God to the test'" (verse 7).

When I was pastoring, some of the members of my church unwittingly yielded to the temptation to put God to the test. I had a dear friend who was dying of cancer. But word spread around the church that four independent "witnesses" all testified that Dick wasn't going to die because God had told them so. Several exclaimed, "Isn't it wonderful that God is going to heal Dick!" Three weeks later Dick was dead.

If God was the One who told these four people that Dick wasn't going to die, what does that make God? A liar. But is God a liar? Of course not; He's the truth. Lies come from the father of lies: Satan himself. Deceiving spirits had circulated a lie about Dick in an attempt to destroy the congregation's confidence in God.

God is under no obligation to us; He is under obligation only to Himself. There is no way you can cleverly word a prayer so that God must respond to it. That not only distorts the meaning of prayer but puts us in the position of God. The righteous shall live by faith in the written Word of God and not demand that God prove Himself in response to our whims or wishes, no matter how noble they may be. We are the ones being tested, not God.

The Pride of Life

The third channel of temptation is at the heart of the New Age movement: the temptation to direct our own destiny, to rule our own world, to be our own god. Satan tantalized Eve concerning the forbidden fruit: "The day you eat from it your eyes will be opened, and you will be like God, knowing good and evil" (Genesis 3:5). Satan's offer was an exaggerated appeal to our God-instilled propensity to rule.."Don't be satisfied ruling *under* God," he seemed to say, "when you have the potential to be *like* God." When Eve was convinced that "the tree was desirable to make one wise" (verse 6), she and Adam ate.

Satan's promise that the couple would become like God was nothing more than a lie. When Adam and Eve yielded to his temptation, they didn't become the gods of this world as he claimed they would. Instead, they fell from their position of rulership with God, and Satan became the god of this world by default—exactly as he had planned.

Satan tried the same ploy with Jesus: "The devil took Him to a very high mountain, and showed Him all the kingdoms of the world and their glory; and he said to Him, 'All these things will I give You if You fall down and worship me'" (Matthew 4:8,9). Jesus didn't challenge Satan's right to offer Him the kingdoms of the world and their glory. Since he was the god of this world, they were his to offer after Adam and Eve forfeited them at the first temptation. When you think about it, however, Satan's offer was pretty ridiculous. Why would Jesus be tempted to worship Satan in exchange for the world when He already owned the universe? So He replied, "Begone, Satan! For it is written, 'You shall worship the Lord your God, and serve Him only'" (verse 10).

The temptation of the pride of life is intended to steer us away from the worship of God and destroy our obedience to God by urging us to take charge of our own lives. Whenever you feel that you don't need God's help or direction, that you can handle your life without consulting Him, that you don't need to bow the knee to anyone, beware: That's the pride of life. You may think you are serving yourself, but whenever you stop worshiping and serving God you are in reality worshiping and serving Satan—which is what he wants more than anything else. Instead, your life should be characterized by worshipful humility and obedience to God (1 Peter 5:5-11; John 15:8-10).

Remember, there are three critical issues reflected in these channels of temptation: 1) the will of God in your life, as expressed through your dependence on God; 2) the Word of God in your life, as expressed through your confidence in God; and 3) the worship of God in your life, as expressed through your obedience to God. Every temptation that Satan throws at you will challenge one or more of these values. He will watch you to learn where you are most vulnerable and will tempt you in any area that you leave unguarded.

TWO OF OUR BIGGEST APPETITES

Why do we entertain tempting thoughts which are contrary to God's Word and God's will? Let's face it—we do so because we want to. We're not tempted by foods we don't like, by unattractive members of the opposite sex, by unwanted promotions, etc. Temptation's hook is the devil's guarantee that what we think we want and need outside God's will can satisfy us. Don't believe it. You can never satisfy the desires of the flesh. Instead, "Blessed are they who hunger and thirst for righteousness, for they shall be satisfied" (Matthew 5:6). Only sustaining right relationships, living by the power of the Holy Spirit, and experiencing the fruit of the Spirit will satisfy you.

Eat to Live or Live to Eat?

Food is the ultimate appetite, since it is necessary for

survival. So we eat to live, but when we begin to live to eat, food no longer satisfies. Instead, it consumes us, and millions of people feel powerless to control their appetite for food. When your body is deprived of necessary nutrients, you naturally crave those foods which will keep you healthy and keep your immune system functioning. If you eat to satisfy those natural cravings you will stay healthy and free. But when you turn to food to relieve anxiety or satisfy a lust for sweets, salt, etc., you will lose control, and the results will negatively affect your health.

It is no coincidence that Paul mentioned misuse of food in conjunction with his sober warning that "in later times some will fall away from the faith, paying attention to deceitful spirits and doctrines of demons" (1 Timothy 4:1). One of the evidences of the last days will be those who "advocate abstaining from foods" (verse 3) which are intended to meet a legitimate need. Every eating disorder I have dealt with had a spiritual component, yet virtually no counselors treating anorexia and bulimia expose the spiritual problem. A pastor's wife wrote to me after a conference:

> Dear Neil,
>
> I can't begin to tell you all that the Lord has done in my life through the truth you shared with us at the conference. I am now more aware of the deception of the enemy, and this makes my gratefulness for my powerful and gracious Savior real. I was bulimic for 11 years. But now I can be in the house alone all day with a kitchen full of food and be in peace. When a temptation or lie from Satan pops into my mind, I fend it off quickly with the truth. I used to be in bondage to those lies for hours and hours each day, always fearing food. Now I'm rejoicing in the freedom which the truth brings.

Sexual Passions Unleashed

Paul also mentioned marriage (the relationship in which God intended the appetite for sex to be fulfilled) in his sober warning about the last days (1 Timothy 4:3). Sex is another stronghold identified in Scripture which holds unique potential for sin. Paul wrote, "Every other sin that a man commits is outside his body, but the immoral man [fornicator] sins against his own body" (1 Corinthians 6:18). Virtually every person I have counseled regarding a spiritual conflict has confessed some kind of sexual aberration. Some were in bondage to uncontrollable lust. Others were the victims of demonic sexual attack. Furthermore, people who were sexually molested or involved in disgusting satanic sex rituals in the past almost always have strongholds in the area of sex. If there is such a thing as demonic transference from one person to another, I would say that illicit sexual union is the chief means by which it happens.

Sex is a God-given part of our autonomic nervous system. Normal sexual functioning is a regular, rhythmic part of life. But when Jesus said, "Everyone who looks on a woman to lust for her has committed adultery with her already in his heart" (Matthew 5:28), he was describing something beyond the boundary of God's design for sex. The word for lust is *epithumos*. The prefix *epi* means "to add to," signifying that something is being added to a normal drive. Jesus challenged us not to add onto the God-given sexual drive by polluting our minds with lustful thoughts. The only way to control your sexual life is to control your thought life.

Sexual lust demands physical expression, and that's where Romans 6 comes into play. We are not to let sin reign in our mortal bodies (verse 12) by using our bodies as instruments of unrighteousness (verse 13). Whenever you use your body wrongly through a sexual offense you give Satan a foothold, and your sexual problem becomes a spiritual problem. A missionary shared with me at the end of a conference that he was finally free after 20 years of bondage to lust. He

sought counseling for his problem during his preparation
for missionary service and on every furlough, but he never
gained lasting victory until he realized that it was a spiritual problem which needed a spiritual solution.

THE WAY OF ESCAPE

First Corinthians 10:13 is the shining good news in midst
of our fears and concerns about temptation: "No temptation has overtaken you but such as is common to man; and
God is faithful, who will not allow you to be tempted
beyond what you are able, but with the temptation will
provide the way of escape also, that you may be able to
endure it." Where is the escape hatch that Paul is talking
about here? In the same place temptation is introduced: in
your mind. Every temptation is first a thought introduced
to your mind by your own carnality or the tempter himself.
If you ruminate on that thought and consider it an option,
you will eventually act on it, and that's sin. Instead Paul
instructs us to take every thought captive to the obedience
of Christ (2 Corinthians 10:5). The first step for escaping
temptation is to apprehend every thought as soon as it steps
through the doorway of your mind.

Once you have halted a penetrating thought, the next
step is to evaluate it on the basis of Paul's eightfold criterion
for what we should think about: "Whatever is true, whatever is honorable, whatever is right, whatever is pure,
whatever is lovely, whatever is of good repute, if there is any
excellence and if anything worthy of praise, let your mind
dwell on these things" (Philippians 4:8). Ask yourself, "Does
this thought line up with God's truth? Is it suggesting that I
do something honorable? Right? Pure? If this thought
becomes action, will the outcome be lovely and contribute
to excellence in my life? Will other believers approve of my
actions? Is it something for which I can praise God?" If the
answer to any of those questions is no, dismiss that thought

immediately. Don't have anything more to do with it. If it keeps coming back, keep saying no. When you learn to respond to tempting thoughts by stopping them at the door of your mind, evaluating them on the basis of God's Word, and dismissing those which fail the test, you have found the way of escape that God's Word promises.

In contrast, if a thought enters your mind and it passes the Philippians 4:8 test of truth, honor, righteousness, etc., "let your mind dwell on these things" (verse 8) and "practice these things" (verse 9). "And the God of peace shall be with you" (verse 9), which is an infinitely better result than the pain and turmoil which follows when we yield to tempting thoughts and become involved in sinful behavior.

Confess and Resist

People who are caught in the sin-confess-sin-confess-sin-confess cycle eventually begin to lose hope that they can experience any real victory over sin. Sheer willpower can't keep them from repeating the sin they just confessed, and Satan pours on the condemnation. Self-control seems like an illusion, and the Christian life is one of unending ups and downs.

Sin which is allowed to reign is like a dog that breaks into your yard, bites you on the leg, and won't let go. You beat on yourself for your failure and cry out to God for forgiveness. He forgives you, but the dog is still there. Why not cry out to God and beat on the dog instead of yourself? James 4:7 tells us, "Submit therefore to God. Resist the devil and he will flee from you." We are correct in confessing our sin, but we have failed to follow the biblical formula which breaks the cycle: sin-confess-*resist*. We must resist Satan and command him to leave if we are going to experience victory over sin.

We live as though God and a sick humanity are the only realities in the spiritual realm. But John wrote: "My little children, I am writing these things to you that you may not sin. And if anyone sins, we have an Advocate with the

Father, Jesus Christ the righteous" (1 John 2:1). We must turn to our righteous Advocate and resist our perverted adversary if we are to experience victory and freedom over temptation and sin.

9

Don't Believe Everything You Hear

One of the most common attitudes I have discovered in Christians—even among pastors, Christian leaders, and their wives and children—is a deep-seated sense of self-deprecation. I've heard them say, "I'm not important, I'm not qualified, I'm no good." I'm amazed at how many Christians are paralyzed in their witness and productivity by thoughts and feelings of inferiority and worthlessness.

Next to temptation, perhaps the most frequent and insistent attack from Satan to which we are vulnerable is accusation. By faith we have entered into an eternal relationship with the Lord Jesus Christ. As a result, we are dead to sin and alive to God, and we now sit with Christ in the heavenlies. In Christ we *are* important, we *are* qualified, we *are* good. Satan can do absolutely nothing to alter our position in Christ and our worth to God. But he can render us virtually inoperative if he can deceive us into listening to and believing his insidious lies accusing us of being of little value to God or other people.

Satan often uses temptation and accusation as a brutal one-two punch. He comes along and says, "Why don't you try it? Everybody does it. Besides, you can get away with it. Who's going to know?" Then as soon as we fall for his tempting line, he changes his tune to accusation: "What kind of a Christian are you to do such a thing? You're a pitiful excuse for a child of God. You'll never get away with it. You might as well give up because God has already given up on you."

Satan is called "the accuser of the brethren . . . who accuses them before our God day and night" (Revelation 12:10). We have all heard his lying, hateful voice in our hearts and consciences. He never seems to let up on us. Many Christians are perpetually discouraged and defeated because they believe his persistent lies about them. And those who give in to his accusations end up being robbed of the freedom that God intends His people to enjoy. One defeated Christian wrote:

> My old feelings that life isn't worth the trouble keep coming back. I'm scared, lonely, confused, and very desperate. I know deep down that God can overcome this, but I can't get past this block. I can't even pray. When I try, things get in my way. When I'm feeling good and I begin putting into action what I know God wants me to do, I'm stopped dead in my tracks by those voices and a force so strong I can't continue. I'm so close to giving in to those voices that I almost can't fight them anymore. I just want some peace.

PUTTING THE ACCUSER IN HIS PLACE

The good news is that we don't have to listen to Satan's accusations and live in despair and defeat. Zechariah 3:1-10 provides the essential truth we need in order to stand by faith against Satan's accusations and to live righteously in the service of God.

The Lord revealed to the prophet Zechariah a heavenly scene in which Satan's accusations of God's people are put into proper perspective: "Then he showed me Joshua the high priest standing before the angel of the Lord, and Satan standing at his right hand to accuse him. And the Lord said to Satan, 'The Lord rebuke you, Satan! Indeed, the Lord who has chosen Jerusalem rebuke you! Is this not a brand plucked from the fire?' Now Joshua was clothed with filthy garments and standing before the angel" (verses 1-3).

The Lord Rebukes Satan

Look at the cast of characters in this scene which resembles a heavenly courtroom. The judge is God the Father. The prosecuting attorney is Satan. The defense attorney is Jesus. And the accused defendant is Joshua the high priest, who represents all of God's people, including you and me. Historically, when the high priest entered God's presence in the holy of holies each year, it was a very solemn occasion. The priest had to perform elaborate purification rites and ceremonial cleansings before entering, because if somehow he wasn't just right before God he could be struck dead on the spot. The priest wore bells on the hem of his robe so those outside the holy of holies could tell if he was still alive and moving. A rope was tied around his ankle so he could be dragged out of the inner sanctuary if he died in God's presence.

So here is a high priest named Joshua standing in God's presence with filthy garments representing the sins of Israel. Bad news! Satan the accuser says, "Look at him, God. He's filthy. He deserves to be struck dead." But God rebukes the accuser and puts him in his place. "You're not the judge, and you cannot pass sentence on my people," God seems to say in His rebuke. "I have rescued Joshua from the flames of judgment, and your accusations are groundless."

This courtroom scene continues night and day for every child of God. Satan persists in pointing out our faults and weaknesses to God and demands that He zap us for being less than perfect. But our defense attorney in heaven is Jesus Christ, and He has never lost a case before God the judge. Satan can't make his charges stick because Jesus Christ has justified us and lives to intercede for us (Romans 8:33,34).

At the same time Satan accuses us before God, and his emissaries also accuse us personally by bombarding our minds with false thoughts of unworthiness and unrighteousness in God's sight: "How could you do that and be a

Christian? You're not really a child of God." But Satan is not your judge; he is merely your *accuser*. Yet if you listen to him and believe him, you will begin to live out these accusations as if they were a sentence you must serve.

When Satan's accusations of unworthiness attack you, don't pay attention to them. Instead respond, "Satan, I have put my trust in Christ, and I am a child of God in Him. Like Joshua the high priest, I have been rescued by God from the fire of judgment, and He has declared me righteous. You cannot determine a verdict or pronounce a sentence. All you can do is accuse me—and I don't buy it."

The Lord Removes Our Filthy Garments

The reason Satan's accusations are groundless is because God has solved the problem of our filthy garments. Zechariah's description of the heavenly scene continues: "And he spoke and said to those who were standing before him saying, 'Remove the filthy garments from him.' Again he said to him, 'See, I have taken your iniquity away from you and will clothe you with festal robes.' Then I said, 'Let them put a clean turban on his head.' So they put a clean turban on his head and clothed him with garments, while the angel of the Lord was standing by" (3:4,5).

God has not only declared us righteous, but He has removed our filthy garments of unrighteousness and clothed us with His righteousness. Notice that the change of wardrobe is something that *God* does, not we ourselves. In ourselves we don't have any garments of righteousness to put on that will satisfy God. He must change us in response to our submission to Him in faith.

The Lord Admonishes Us to Respond

Having rebuked Satan and provided our righteousness, the Lord calls for a response of obedience: "If you will walk in My ways, and if you will perform My service, then you will also govern My house and also have charge of My courts, and I will grant you free access among these who are standing here" (Zechariah 3:7). God's condition here has nothing to do with your relationship with Him or your standing of righteousness, since they are already secure. And these admonitions have nothing to do with Satan's defeat, since he is already defeated. They have to do with your *daily victory*. In calling us to walk in His ways and perform His service, the Lord is simply calling us to live out our identity in Christ through our practical expressions of obedience. This means living by faith instead of fear. It means crucifying the flesh on a daily basis and walking according to the Spirit. It means considering ourselves dead to sin and alive to God and not allowing sin to reign in our mortal bodies. It means taking every thought captive to the obedience of Christ and being transformed by the renewing of our minds.

In response to our daily ministry to Him through obedience, God promises that we will govern His house and have charge of His courts. This means that we will share in His authority in the spiritual world, able to live victoriously over Satan and sin. He also promises us free access in the heavenlies. We have an open line of communication with the Father. As we operate in His authority and live in fellowship and harmony with Him, our daily victory and fruitfulness are assured.

RECOGNIZING A CRITICAL DIFFERENCE

You may wonder, "What's the difference between the devil's accusations and the Holy Spirit's conviction?" Paul provided a clear distinction between the two in 2 Corinthians 7:9,10: "I now rejoice, not that you were made sorrowful, but that you were made sorrowful to the point of repentance; for you were made sorrowful according to the will of God, in order that you might not suffer loss in anything through us. For the sorrow that is according to the will of God produces a repentance without regret, leading to salvation; but the sorrow of the world produces death."

The worldly system and the Holy Spirit's conviction both produce the feeling of sorrow. However, the sorrow resulting from Satan's accusation leads to death, while the sorrow of conviction is a sorrow designed to provoke repentance which leads to life. Paul wasn't rejoicing that the Corinthians felt sorrowful; he was rejoicing that their sorrow would lead to repentance, a knowledge of the truth, and finally freedom.

Every Christian is faced with the choice of walking by the Spirit or by the flesh on a daily basis. The moment you choose to walk according to the flesh, the Holy Spirit brings conviction because what you have just chosen to do is not compatible with who you really are. If you continue in the flesh you will feel the sorrow of conviction.

"How do I know which kind of sorrow I'm experiencing?" you may ask. "They feel the same." Determine whether your feelings reflect thoughts of truth or error, and you will identify their source. Do you feel guilty, worthless, stupid, or inept? That's a sorrow provoked by accusation because those feelings don't reflect truth. Judicially, you are no longer guilty; you have been justified through your faith in Christ, and there is no condemnation for those who are in Christ. You are not worthless; Jesus gave His life for you. You are not stupid or inept; you can do all things through Christ. When you find lies lurking beneath your feelings of sorrow—especially if your feelings persistently drive you into the ground—you are being falsely accused. Even if you changed you wouldn't feel any better, because Satan would then find something else to harass you about. To disarm the sorrow of accusation you must submit yourself to God and resist the devil and his lies.

But if you are sorrowful because your behavior doesn't reflect your true identity in Christ, that's the sorrow according to the will of God which is designed to produce repentance. It's the Holy Spirit calling you to admit on the basis of 1 John 1:9, "Dear Lord, I was wrong." As soon as you confess and repent, God says, "I'm glad you shared that with Me. You're cleansed; now get on with life." And you walk away from that confrontation free. The sorrow is gone, and you have a positive new resolve to obey God in the area of your failure.

A graphic example of the contrast between accusation and conviction is found in the lives of Judas Iscariot and Simon Peter. Somehow Judas allowed Satan to deceive him into betraying Jesus for 30 pieces of silver (Luke 22:3-5). When Judas realized what he had done, he was so remorseful that he hung himself. Was his suicide the result of Satan's accusation or of God's conviction? It had to be accusation because it drove Judas to kill himself. Accusation leads to death; conviction leads to repentance and life.

Peter also failed Jesus by denying Him. It apparently began with pride as the disciples argued over who was the greatest among them (Luke 22:24-30). Jesus told Peter, "Simon, Simon, behold, Satan has demanded permission to sift you like wheat" (verse 31). That's right—Jesus allowed Satan to put Peter through the mill because Peter had given the enemy a foothold through pride. But Jesus also looked at Peter and said, "I have prayed for you, that your faith may not fail; and you, when once you have turned again, strengthen your brothers" (verse 32).

Peter vowed to die with Jesus, but Jesus told him that he would deny Him three times (verses 33,34), which he did. The remorse Peter felt was every bit as painful as that which Judas experienced. But Peter's sorrow was from conviction which led to his eventual repentance and restoration to Christ (John 21:15-17). When your feelings of remorse pound you into the ground and drive you from God, you are being accused by Satan. Resist it. But when your sorrow draws you to confront Christ and confess your wrong, you are being convicted by the Spirit. Yield to it through repentance.

According to Revelation 12:10, Satan's continuing work is to accuse the brethren. But the good news is that Christ's continuing work is to intercede for us as He did for Peter.

The writer of Hebrews declared, "He is able to save forever those who draw near to God through Him, since He always lives to make intercession for them" (7:25). We have a persistent adversary, but we have an even more persistent, eternal advocate who defends us before the Father on the basis of our faith in Him (1 John 2:1).

THE QUICKSAND OF ACCUSATION

How important is it that we learn to resist the persistent accusations of Satan? It is absolutely vital to our daily victory in Christ. We have all felt like worthless nobodies from time to time. And when we feel like worthless nobodies we act like worthless nobodies, and our lives and ministries suffer until we resist Satan and return to a life of victory. But Satan never gives up. He will try to get us down more often and keep us down longer by hurling one false accusation after another. If we fail to keep resisting him we may become vulnerable to even more serious attacks from Satan. Janelle's story is an extreme case, but it illustrates what can happen to a Christian who fails to take a stand against the accuser of the brethren.

Janelle was a Christian woman with severe emotional problems who was brought to me by her elderly pastor. Janelle's fiancé, Curt, came with them. After introducing me to Janelle and Curt, the pastor started to leave. "Wait a minute," I said. "I'd prefer that you stay with us."

"I've got a bad heart," the pastor replied. He may have had heart trouble, but I really think he was fearful that our session might get a little bizarre.

"I don't think anything will happen here today that will affect your heart," I assured. (Little did I realize what was about to happen!) "Besides, you're her pastor, and I would appreciate your prayer support." The pastor reluctantly agreed.

As Janelle told me her story I realized that the accuser of the brethren had really done a number on her. She had been the victim of one abuse after another as a child and adolescent. Her background also included a sick relationship with a previous boyfriend who was involved in the occult. Over the years she had come to believe Satan's lies that she was the cause of her troubles and that she was of no value to God or anybody else. Her self-perception was down in the mud.

Recognizing Satan's familiar strategy, I said, "Janelle, we can help you with your problems because there is a battle going on for your mind which God has given us authority to win." As soon as I spoke those words Janelle suddenly went catatonic. She sat as still as a stone, eyes glazed over and staring into space.

"Have you ever seen her behave like this?" I asked her pastor and fiancé.

"No," they answered, wide-eyed. They were more than a little frightened.

"Well, there's nothing to worry about. I've seen it before," I said. "We're going to take authority over it, but it's important that you two affirm your right standing with God in order to prevent any transference of this demonic influence."

I led the pastor in a prayer similar to those found in Chapter 12. When I turned to lead Curt in prayer, he started to shake. "Curt, is there something between you and God that's not right? If so, I suggest you get it cleared up right now." Under the circumstances, Curt didn't need much prompting! He began confessing sin in his life, including the revelation that he and Janelle had been sleeping together. In response to my counsel, Curt committed himself to end that practice. All the while Janelle sat motionless, totally blanked out.

After we had prayed together about getting his life straight with God, I gave Curt a sheet of paper with a prayer on it to read. As soon as Curt began to read the prayer, Janelle snapped to life. She let out a menacing growl, then lashed out and slapped the paper out of Curt's hands. Satan tried to use the suddenness of her actions to frighten us, and for an instant it *was* frightening. But it was just another of his scare tactics prompting us to react in fear. I addressed the demonic influence in Janelle: "In the name of Christ and by His authority, I bind you to that chair and I command you to sit there."

I wish I could have videotaped my encounter with Janelle that day in order to show the skeptics what happens when Satan's attempt is confronted by God's authority. It was as if Wonder Woman had lassoed Janelle and tied her to the chair. She just sat there squirming, bound to the chair by the ropes of God's authority. Her eyes blazed at Curt with hatred, which was further evidence of the demonic power which was controlling her. Janelle didn't hate Curt; she loved him. They were going to be married. But Satan hated the fact that his strongholds in Curt and Janelle were being torn down, and his hatred was mirrored in Janelle's countenance.

Curt finished reading the prayer while Janelle continued to squirm in her chair. Then I prayed, "Lord, we declare our dependence on You, for apart from Christ we can do nothing. Now, in the name and authority of the Lord Jesus Christ, we command Satan and all his forces to release Janelle and to remain bound within her so she will be free to obey God her heavenly Father." Suddenly Janelle slumped in her chair and snapped out of her catatonic state.

"Do you remember anything we've been doing here?" I asked her.

"No, what happened?" she responded with a puzzled expression.

"It's nothing to worry about," I told her. "Somehow Satan has gained a foothold in your life. But we would like to walk you through the steps to freedom in Christ." About an hour later Janelle was free.

What right did Satan have to control Janelle as he did? Only the right that she gave him by yielding to his lies. Satan had convinced her that she was of little value and that what she did was of little consequence. So she lived on the fringe of immorality and dabbled in the occult, allowing Satan even greater access, to the point of partial control. But once Janelle renounced her involvement with sin and Satan, his hold on her was canceled, and he had to leave.

For most of us, Satan's deceptive accusations will not result in the kind of bondage illustrated by Janelle's experience. But if he can cause you to doubt your worth to God or your effectiveness as His child through his accusations, he can neutralize your life for God. Put your feelings to the test. Take every thought captive. Don't believe anything Satan says about you; it's a lie. Believe everything God says about you; it's the truth which will set you free.

10

Appearances Can Be Deceiving

I had just finished speaking at a Sunday evening service in a church in San Diego, when a friend of mine who attended there passed me a note: "I brought a family to church with me tonight. Will you please see them before you leave?" I was dead tired from a weekend of speaking, and I still had at least an hour of ministry ahead of me with people who wanted to talk after the service. But I agreed to see the family if they could wait until I was finished.

Unknown to me, my friend had practically dragged 26-year-old Alyce and her parents to the service against their will. They were Christians, but as I sat down with them it was obvious that they had a problem. Alyce was one of the most pathetic-looking young women I have ever met. She was so skinny that she literally had no more body fat to lose. She had lost her job three days earlier, and her vacant eyes conveyed that she had lost all hope for her life.

Alyce's father told me that she had suffered terribly from PMS during adolescence and had become addicted to prescription painkillers. She was a very talented girl and a committed Christian in many ways, but she was also a Darvon junkie who had even been arrested once for illegal possession of prescription drugs. As her father told me her sad story, Alyce sat nodding to herself as if to say, "Yes, that's me, and life is the pits."

Finally I turned to Alyce, took her by the hands, and said, "I want you to tell me who you think you are."

"I'm just a no-good failure," she whimpered.

153

"You're not a failure," I responded. "You're a child of God." She continued to pour out the negative self-talk and evidences of demonic deception she had been living under, and I continued to counter her negativism with the good news of her identity in Christ. The hour was late and I was tired, but the more we talked the more aware I became of Christ's presence ministering to Alyce. We tested the spirit that was harassing her in these areas, and she saw firsthand that she had been subject to a demonic influence.

Finally she said, "Do you mean to tell me that all these negative thoughts about myself are nothing but satanic deception?"

"That's right, Alyce," I nodded. "And as you begin to learn the truth about your identity in Christ, you will be free from the bondage of Satan's lies."

Two weeks later Alyce was enrolled in an intensive 12-week, live-in spiritual growth course at the Julian Center near San Diego. At the end of the course Alyce began to take the initiative in her life instead of remaining the victim of Satan's deception. She got a job and gained about 25 pounds. And today she's free.

The prevailing theme of the New Testament is the position we enjoy in Christ through our faith in Him. That's the good news: Christ in you and you in Christ. If there is a prevailing negative theme in the New Testament which capsulizes the opposition we face in Satan, I believe it is deception. I encourage you to do a word search through an exhaustive concordance to see how many times the words deceive, deceived, and deception are used in the New Testament. You will discover that Satan's worldwide work is characterized repeatedly by this concept.

There are at least three avenues through which Satan will attempt to dissuade you from God's truth and deceive you into believing his lies: self-deception, false prophets/teachers, and deceiving spirits. We are vulnerable to Satan's deception in these areas if we fail to clothe ourselves daily with the spiritual armor of the belt of truth.

BEWARE OF SELF-DECEPTION

Is it really possible for Christians to deceive themselves? Yes, it is very possible. The Scriptures reveal several patterns of behavior through which Christians become vulnerable to self-deception.

We deceive ourselves when we hear the Word but don't do it (James 1:22; 1 Peter 1:13). I am learning about pastors and missionaries across the country who are preaching against the very sins they are committing themselves. Nationally known Christian personalities who vehemently condemn immorality have themselves been found to be hiding an immoral lifestyle. Those of us who are called to preach or teach God's Word must put it on first. We must get on our knees before God as we prepare the message and say, "God, is this Scripture true in my life?" If not, we had better be honest enough to say to those who hear us, "I wish I were a better example of this passage than I am, but I'm still growing in this area." To proclaim the Word of God as if it were true in your life when it's not is a lie, and you are participating in the deception by deceiving yourself.

Those of us who receive the Word are also vulnerable to self-deception if we fail to put it into practice. We hear a sermon or a lesson and say, "Wow! What a great truth!" and hurry off to share it with someone else without processing it ourselves and applying it to our own lives. James said that hearers of the Word who are not also doers of the Word deceive themselves (1:22).

Why are we afraid to admit it when our lives don't completely match up to Scripture? I believe it's because many of us have a perfection complex. We think we have to model perfection and not admit to failure. But we can't model perfection because we're not perfect; we can only model *growth.* The people around us need to know that we are real people in the process of maturing. They need to see how we handle failure as well as how we handle success. When we model this kind of honesty in the Christian community we greatly reduce the possibility of the deceiver gaining a foothold.

We deceive ourselves when we say we have no sin (1 John 1:8). The Scripture doesn't say that we *are* sin; it says that it is possible for us to sin and for sin to reside in our mortal bodies (Romans 6:12). We are not sinless saints; we are saints who occasionally sin. It's important to keep honest account of our failures and pick up our cross daily. When we become aware of a discrepancy between our identity and our behavior, we must confess it and deal with it. The person who deceives himself by ignoring these sinful discrepancies and allowing them to build up is headed for a great fall.

Those of us who live in earthquake-prone Southern California keep hearing about "the big one," which is thought by many to be inevitable along the San Andreas fault. Whenever we experience minor earthquakes (up to about four on the Richter scale), we may be frightened by them a bit, but we also see them as a good sign. These little temblors mean that the plates in the earth's crust beneath us are shifting. As long as the crust is adjusting this way it's unlikely that "the big one" will hit. It's when we don't get any minor earthquakes for several months or years that the danger of a major, devastating quake increases.

Living in the light, holding ourselves accountable to God, and confessing and dealing with sin on a daily basis prevents the major spiritual crises from building up in our lives. If we keep saying, "I don't have any sin," or if we fail to acknowledge our shortcomings and settle our differences with people as God convicts us of them, we're in for "the big one." We will eventually lose our health, our family, our job, or our friendships. Unacknowledged sin is like a cancer which will grow to consume us.

We deceive ourselves when we think we are something we are not (Romans 12:3; Galatians 6:3). The Scriptures instruct us not to think of ourselves more highly than we ought to think. "But I know who I am," you say. "I'm a child of God, I'm seated with Christ in the heavenlies, I can do all things through Him. That makes me pretty special." Yes, you are very special in the eyes of God. But you are what you are by the grace of God (1 Corinthians 15:10). The life you live, the talents you possess, and the gifts you have received are not personal accomplishments; they are expressions of God's grace. Never take credit for what God has provided; rather, take delight in accomplishing worthwhile deeds which glorify the Lord.

We deceive ourselves when we think we are wise in this age (1 Corinthians 3:18,19). It is the height of intellectual arrogance to assume wisdom without the revelation of God. "Professing to be wise, they became fools" (Romans 1:22). Sometimes we are tempted to think we can match wits and intellect with the god of this world. But we are no match for him. Whenever we think we can outsmart Satan on our own, we are prime candidates to be led astray by his craftiness. However, Satan is no match for God. It is important for us not to lean on our own understanding, but to employ the mind of Christ and acknowledge Him in all our ways (Proverbs 3:5,6; 1 Corinthians 2:16).

We deceive ourselves when we think we are religious but do not bridle our tongue (James 1:26). There is nothing that grieves God more than when we bad-mouth people instead of building them up with our speech. We are never to use our tongues to put others down. Instead we are to edify one another in what we say and thereby give grace to those who hear us. If your tongue is out of control, you're fooling yourself to believe that you have your spiritual life together.

We deceive ourselves when we think we will not reap what we sow (Galatians 6:7). As Christians we sometimes think we are exempt from this principle, but we are not. We will have to live with the results and consequences of our thoughts, words, and actions, whether good or bad.

We deceive ourselves when we think the unrighteous will inherit the kingdom of God (1 Corinthians 6:9,10). Kate, a young woman who was interning at a church I served, walked into the office one day completely devastated. She had just learned that her older sister, who had led her to Christ, had walked away from God and was living in a lesbian relationship. "My lifestyle doesn't make any difference," Kate's sister had argued. "God loves me and I'm forgiven." Kate was distraught and confused.

I directed her to 1 Corinthians 6: "Do not be deceived; neither fornicators, nor idolaters, nor adulterers, nor effeminate, nor homosexuals . . . shall inherit the kingdom of God" (verses 9,10). Somehow Kate's sister and others like her are deceived, failing to understand this truth: Living a brazenly sinful life is strong evidence of an unrighteous standing before God. This is not a works gospel; it is a matter of identifying true disciples by their fruit. You are absolutely deceived if you believe that your lifestyle does not need to line up with your profession.

We deceive ourselves when we think we can continually associate with bad company and not be corrupted (1 Corinthians 15:33). When I was a young Christian I used to listen to records by an evangelist in New Orleans who was called "the Bourbon Street preacher." This man lived in the red light district and claimed to have a ministry to prostitutes and other questionable characters. But according to 1 Corinthians 15:33, anyone who stays in that environment too long will get into trouble. And that's just what happened to this evangelist. He became so entangled with the seedy side of Bourbon Street that he eventually lost his ministry.

Does this mean that we shouldn't minister to those with bad morals? No, we must share Christ with them. But if we immerse ourselves in their environment, our ministry will eventually diminish and our morality will be affected for the worse.

BEWARE OF FALSE PROPHETS AND TEACHERS

Recently a man in his thirties was referred to me. Alvin was discouraged and defeated. For several years he believed he had a special gift of prophecy from God. He was invited to church after church to speak as an oracle for God by prophesying in his unique way. But over a period of months his personal life began to fall apart. Alvin eventually reached the point where he could no longer function in society, and he began to withdraw from people completely. By the time he came to see me he had been unemployed for two years, he was being cared for by his father, and he was a slave to prescription drugs.

Alvin and I read 1 Thessalonians 5:19-21: "Do not put out the Spirit's fire; do not treat prophecies with contempt. Test everything. Hold on to the good" (NIV). I said, "Alvin, I'm not against prophecy; it's a spiritual gift. But Satan can counterfeit spiritual gifts and deceive us into believing they're from God. That's why the Scriptures instruct us to put everything to the test."

After a lengthy discussion about false prophets and teachers, Alvin admitted, "I think my problems began when I failed to test the 'gifts' of tongues and prophecy conferred on me by false teachers. Not only was I deceived, but I have deceived others myself."

"Would you be willing to put your gift of tongues to the test?" I asked. I assured Alvin that I was interested in putting the spirit to the test, not him.

Alvin really wanted to be free of deception and right with God. "Yes," he answered.

I instructed Alvin to begin praying aloud in his "spiritual language." As he began to chant an unintelligible prayer, I said, "In the name of Christ and in obedience to God's Word, I command you, spirit, to identify yourself."

Alvin stopped in the middle of his chanting and said, "I am he."

At this point a novice may have been tempted to take off his shoes, thinking he was on holy ground. But I continued the test: "Are you the 'he' who was crucified under Pontius Pilate, buried, raised on the third day, and who now sits at the right hand of the Father?"

Alvin almost shouted the response: "No! Not he!" I led Alvin through a prayer renouncing Satan's activity in his life, and he was free from that deception.

I am not against spiritual gifts, even prophesy and tongues. I am committed to obeying Scripture, and 1 Corinthians 14:39 says, "Desire earnestly to prophesy, and do not forbid to speak in tongues." But Scripture also requires that all spiritual phenomena be tested. I believe that false prophets and teachers flourish today simply because Christians accept their ministry without testing the spirits behind it.

Comparing the Counterfeit with the Real

Every true prophet of God in the Old Testament was an evangelist. His ministry drew people back to God and His Word. The call to righteousness was the standard which separated the genuine prophet from the imitation. Jeremiah wrote: "Thus says the Lord of hosts, 'Do not listen to the words of the prophets who are prophesying to you.... I did not send these prophets, but they ran. I did not speak to them, but they prophesied. But if they had stood in My council, then they would have announced My words to My people, and would have turned them back from their evil way and from the evil of their deeds'" (23:16,21,22). If you come across someone who claims to be a prophet, but who is not involved in calling people to a righteous walk with God, you may be dealing with a counterfeit.

The Lord revealed through Jeremiah another criterion for distinguishing a true prophet from a false prophet:

"I have heard what the prophets have said who prophesy falsely in My name, saying, 'I had a dream, I had a dream!' . . . The prophet who has a dream may relate his dream, but let him who has My word speak My word in truth. What does straw have in common with grain?" (verses 25,28). God is warning His people against prophets who value their dreams above His Word.

God is not saying that dreams are unimportant. Indeed, He often spoke to people in the Bible through dreams. But in comparison to the nutritious grain of His Word, dreams are mere straw. If you feed straw to cattle, they'll die. They will sleep on it, but they won't eat it because it has no nutrients. Similarly, dreams are of some value, but they are never to be equated with God's Word as the basis for our faith or our walk. Dreams must be validated and squared against God's Word; it's never the other way around.

Jeremiah continues: " 'Is not my word like fire?' declares the Lord, 'and like a hammer which shatters a rock?' " (23:29). If you attend a Christian fellowship where prophecies are part of public worship, don't expect from God generic drivel like "I love you, my children" or "I'm coming soon." These statements are certainly true, but why would they need to be prophesied, since the Bible already clearly asserts God's love and Christ's imminent return? I have heard "prophecies" like these given in churches where many people were living in sin, lulling them into an unrighteous complacency.

The voice of a prophet should be like a consuming fire and a shattering hammer. A prophetic message should motivate people to righteousness, not placate them in their sin (1 Peter 4:17). God is more concerned about church purity than about church growth. Comfort only comes to those who are persecuted for righteousness' sake by allowing God's Word to purge their sin and shatter their self-centeredness.

Jeremiah relates a couple of other evidences of false prophets: " 'Behold, I am against the prophets,' declares the Lord, 'who steal My words from each other'" (23:30). That's plagiarism: taking what God gave someone else and using it as if it were your own. "'I am against the prophets,' declares the Lord, 'who use their tongues and declare, "The Lord declares"'" (verse 31).

Declaring that what you are saying is directly from the Lord when it isn't, is an incredible offense to God. Has anybody ever come up to you and said, "The Lord told me to tell you..."? My response is, "No, He didn't! If God wants me to know something He can tell me directly." I believe in the priesthood of believers; God can and will encourage us and confirm His Word to us through others. But in matters of faith and direction for your life, "there is one God, and one mediator also between God and men, the man Christ Jesus" (1 Timothy 2:5). If someone says to you "God told me to tell you..." that person is functioning as a medium.

Signs and Wonders: Who's Being Tested?

You may have heard that you can identify a false prophet by the fact that not all his prophecies come true. Deuteronomy 18:22 instructs us not to believe the prophet whose prophesies fail. But Deuteronomy 13:1-3 also warns us about the false prophet whose signs and wonders *do* come true: "If a prophet or a dreamer of dreams arises among you and gives you a sign or a wonder, and the sign or wonder comes true, concerning which he spoke to you, saying, 'Let us go after other gods (whom you have not known) and let us worship them,' you shall not listen to the words of that prophet or that dreamer of dreams; for the Lord your God is testing you to find out if you love the Lord your God with all your heart and with all your soul" (see also Matthew 24:4-11,23-25; Revelation 13:11-14).

Many Christians have become conditioned to think that anything relating to the miraculous automatically verifies that God is involved. God can still use signs and wonders to confirm the Word, but the Bible also warns that "false Christs and false prophets will arise, and will show signs and wonders, in order, if possible, to lead the elect astray" (Mark 13:22). Satan can also perform signs and wonders, but he only does so to direct our worship away from God to himself. Deuteronomy 13:5-11 reveals the seriousness of attributing to God the activity of Satan. Persons who were involved in it were to be executed, even if they were relatives. We are to love God, obey His Word, and test all signs, wonders, and dreams.

Counterfeits in the Church

What comes to mind when you hear the terms "false prophets" and "false teachers"? Many people tend to think of Eastern mystics and gurus, the spokespersons for non-biblical religions, or dynamic cult leaders—people who are recognizably outside the boundaries of the Christian church. But the apostle Peter devoted an entire chapter in one of his letters to false prophets and teachers who operate *within* the church: "But false prophets also arose among the people, just as there will be false teachers among you, who will secretly introduce destructive heresies, even denying the Master who bought them, bringing swift destruction upon themselves" (2 Peter 2:1). These people are in our churches right now, disguised as workers of righteousness.

Notice that the lure of false teachers is not primarily their doctrine: "And many will follow their sensuality, and because of them the way of the truth will be maligned" (verse 2). What does Peter mean by "follow their sensuality"? He is talking about Christians who evaluate a ministry based on the outward appearance and charm of its leaders. We say, "He's such a nice guy"; "She's a very charismatic person"; "He's a real dynamic speaker"; "She's so sweet and sounds so sincere." But is physical attractiveness a biblical criterion for validating a ministry or a teacher? Of course not! The issue is always *truth and righteousness*, and false teachers who appeal to the physical senses have maligned the way of the truth.

Peter goes on to reveal two ways by which we can identify false prophets and false teachers who operate within the church. First, they will be involved in immorality of some kind, indulging "the flesh in its corrupt desires" (verse 10). They may be discovered in illicit activities involving sex and/or money. They may be antinomian, claiming that God is all love and grace so we don't need to abide by any law. Their immorality may not be easy to spot, but it will eventually surface in their lives (2 Corinthians 11:15).

Second, false prophets and teachers "despise authority" and are "daring, self-willed" (2 Peter 2:10). These people have an independent spirit. They do their own thing and won't answer to anybody. They either won't submit to the authority of a denomination or board, or they will pick their own board which will simply rubber-stamp anything they want to do.

There are historic leadership roles in Scripture: prophet (preaching and teaching), priest (pastoring and shepherding), and king (administration). Only Jesus in His perfection is capable of occupying all three roles simultaneously. I believe we need the checks and balances of a plurality of elders in the church, distributing the three critical roles to more than one person. No one can survive his own unchallenged authority. Every true, committed Christian in a leadership role needs to submit himself and his ideas to other mature believers who will hold him accountable. If your pastor is not under authority, or if he doesn't display the heart of a shepherd and a servant, get out of his church.

BEWARE OF DECEIVING SPIRITS

In addition to warning us against self-deception and false prophets and teachers, Scripture warns us against the deception which comes through demonic influence. Paul alerted Timothy: "The Spirit explicitly says that in later times some will fall away from the faith, paying attention to deceitful spirits and doctrines of demons" (1 Timothy 4:1). John also cautioned us to test the spirits in order to unmask Antichrists (1 John 2:18) and to distinguish the spirit of truth from the spirit of error (4:1-6). Satan's demonic forces are at work attempting to pollute your mind with lies in order to keep you from walking in the truth. Hannah Whitehall Smith wrote:

> There are the voices of evil and deceiving spirits, who lie in wait to entrap every traveler entering these higher regions of spiritual life. In the same epistle that tells us that we are seated in the heavenly places in Christ, we are also told that we shall have to fight with spiritual enemies. These spiritual enemies, whoever or whatever they may be, must necessarily communicate with us by means of our spiritual faculties, and their voices, as the voice of God, are an inward impression made upon our spirit. Therefore, just as the Holy Spirit may tell us by impressions what the will of God is concerning us, so also will these spiritual enemies tell us by impression what is their will concerning us, though not, of course, giving it their name.[1]

Due to the deceptive nature of his impressions, Satan's voice may not always be detected objectively. The following is an example of the kind of prayer we need to pray in order to disassociate ourselves from deceiving spirits: "Heavenly Father, I commit myself unreservedly to Your will. If I have been deceived in any way, I pray that You will open my eyes to the deception. I command in the name of the Lord Jesus Christ that all deceiving spirits depart from me, and I renounce and reject all counterfeit gifts (or any other spiritual phenomena). Lord, if it is from You, bless it and cause it to grow that Your body may be blessed and edified through it. Amen."

DISCERNING DECEPTION

True spiritual discernment is nearly a lost practice in evangelical churches. But in reality discernment should be our first line of defense against deception. It's that buzzer which sounds inside warning you that something is wrong. For example, you visit someone's home and everyone is smiling. But you can cut the air with a knife. Even though nothing visible confirms it, your spirit detects that something is amiss in that family.

What is discernment? The first step to understanding discernment is to understand the motive which is essential for employing it. In 1 Kings 3, Israel's king Solomon cries out to God for help. God comes to the king in a dream and asks him what he wants. Solomon responds: "Give Thy servant an understanding heart to judge Thy people to discern between good and evil" (verse 9). God answers: "Because you have asked this thing and have not asked for yourself long life, nor have asked riches for yourself, nor have you asked for the life of your enemies, but have asked for yourself discernment to understand justice, behold, I have done according to your words. Behold, I have given you a wise and discerning heart" (verses 11,12).

The motive for true discernment is never to promote self, to amass personal gain, or to secure an advantage over another person—even an enemy. The Greek word for discernment—*diakrino*—simply means to make a judgment or a distinction. Discernment has only one function: to distinguish right from wrong so the right can be promoted and the wrong can be eliminated. In 1 Corinthians 12:10 discernment is the divinely enabled ability to distinguish a good spirit from a bad spirit. It is one of the gifts of the Spirit which is to be utilized to edify the church.

Discernment is not a function of the mind; it's a function of the Holy Spirit which is in union with your soul/spirit. When the Spirit sounds a warning, your mind, which is designed to deal with clear objectivity, may not be able to perceive what's wrong. In fact, if your mind tries to interpret the warning objectively, you will probably miss the point of the warning. When you discern that something is wrong, simply say to those with you, "I sense that something is out of order here. Let's ask God to help us." Then allow God to bring conviction as only He can.

In many counseling cases I am able to sense in my spirit that something is wrong or that the real issue has not surfaced. Sometimes I seem to know what it is, but instead of blurting it out, I test it. For example, if I discern that the counselee may be in bondage to homosexuality, I don't say, "You're a homosexual, aren't you?" Rather, I test the impression at the appropriate time by saying something like, "Have you ever struggled with homosexual thoughts or tendencies?" If the Spirit's discernment in me is matched by His conviction in the counselee, usually the problem surfaces and is dealt with, setting the captive free.

Satan's counterfeit for discernment is motivated by the desire to serve self instead of edify the church. Lana, an undergraduate student I counseled, was deceived by Satan's version of discernment. She had been seeing another counselor because she was deeply troubled. When she came to see me, Lana explained that she could walk through our campus and point out students who had problems with drugs and sex. She had no hard facts or information; she just "knew." And from what I could tell, she was right. Lana thought she had an unusual gift from God, but she also told me how she would con her counselor by telling him what he was going to do next.

"You like having power over people, don't you, Lana?" I said. The moment I exposed the false spirit it manifested itself in my office in an ugly way. We took authority over the demonic influence and it left her. When she was free she no longer had the "ability" to identify the sins of others. Lana's mind was so quiet that she had to learn to live without the noise from her "companions" which had cluttered her mind for years.

Familiar spirits operate in the demonic realm like the Holy Spirit operates in the Christian realm. Have you ever "known" that someone was a Christian before he or she even said anything about it? Have you ever sensed a compatible spirit with other believers? There is nothing magical about that; it's just the presence of the Holy Spirit bearing witness with your spirit. At other times the Holy Spirit warns you that the spirit controlling another person is not a compatible spirit.

If we would learn to be more spiritually aware in our churches and homes, God could keep us from plowing head-on into so many disasters. In the Western world our cognitive, left-brain orientation all but excludes discernment as our essential guide for navigating through the spiritual world. But the writer of Hebrews identified discernment as the foundation of a good systematic theology: "Solid food is for the mature, who because of practice have their senses trained to discern good and evil" (5:14).

We are more vulnerable to Satan's deception than to any of his other schemes. Why? Because when he tempts you or accuses you, you can recognize it, but when he deceives you, you don't always know it. That's his strategy: to keep you in the dark. If he can get into your church, your home, or your mind undetected, he can control those lives and those ministries. Sad to say, he is doing just that across our land by deceiving many people.

You cannot expose Satan's deception by human reasoning; you can only do it by God's revelation. Jesus said, "If you abide in My word, then you are truly disciples of Mine; and you shall know the truth, and the truth shall make you free" (John 8:31,32). Jesus prayed, "Sanctify them in the truth; Thy word is truth" (John 17:17). It is critical that when you put on the armor of God you start with the belt of truth (Ephesians 6:14). The light of truth is the only valid weapon against the darkness of deception.

I close this chapter with an encouraging letter from a young woman who was trapped in deception until the

Bondage Breaker set her free as we walked through the steps to freedom:

Dear Dr. Anderson:

I will always remember the day I came to you for counsel and prayer. Ever since that day I have felt such freedom. There are no more voices or feelings of heaviness in my brain. I'm even enjoying a physical sense of release. Satan has returned many times trying to clobber me with those old thoughts, but his hold on me has been broken.

I'll never forget what you told me. You said that those negative thoughts about God and myself were lies that Satan planted in my mind. You said I have the power through Jesus Christ to rebuke Satan and get rid of the evil thoughts. It has taken me awhile to really believe that with all my heart, but lately I've decided to fight back—and it works! It's been wonderful to deal with my problems with a clear head. Thank you for helping me and so many others find peace and learn to trust, love, and believe in the Lord.

Love in Christ

11

The Danger of Losing Control

I received the following letter from a young woman I have never met. Sheila attended a Saturday conference I conducted at her church on resolving spiritual conflicts. On Sunday the pastor of the church handed me this letter from her:

Dear Neil,

I have been set free—praise the Lord! Yesterday, for the first time in years, the voices stopped. I could hear the silence. When we sang, I could hear myself sing.

For the first 14 years of my life I lived with an oppressive, abusive mother who never said "I love you" or put her arms around me when I cried. I received no affection, no kind words, no affirmation, no sense of who I was—only physical and emotional abuse. At 15 I was subjected to three weeks of Erhard Seminar Training (EST), which really screwed up my mind. The year which followed was pure hell. My mother threw me out, so I went to live with another family. Eventually they also threw me out.

Three years later I found Christ. My decision to trust Christ was largely based on my fear of Satan and the power of evil I had experienced in my life. Even though I knew Satan had lost his ownership of me, I was unaware of how vulnerable I still was to his deception and control. For the first two years of my Christian life I was in bondage to a sin I didn't even know was a sin. Once I realized my sin, confessed it to

171

God, and received forgiveness, I thought I was finally free of Satan's attempts to control me. I didn't realize that the battle had only begun.

I suffered from unexplainable rashes, hives, and welts all over my body. I lost my joy and closeness to the Lord. I could no longer sing or quote Scripture. I turned to food as my comfort and security. The demons attacked my sense of right and wrong, and I became involved in immorality in my search for identity and love.

But that all ended yesterday when I renounced Satan's control in my life. I have found the freedom and protection which comes from knowing I am loved. I'm not on a high; I'm writing with a clear mind, a clean spirit, and a calm hand. Even my previous bondage to food seems suddenly foreign to me.

I never realized that a Christian could be so vulnerable to Satan's control. I was deceived, but now I am free. Thank you, thank you, Jesus!

—Sheila

Sheila is a sobering example of a dimension of spiritual vulnerability that most Christians don't like to talk about: demonic control. As a believer, Sheila had obviously lost control in her eating habits, in her sexual behavior, and in her devotional life. She wasn't growing spiritually; she was shrinking. She didn't sing and read Scripture because she *couldn't* sing and read Scripture. She was blocked from doing so because of spiritual bondage.

We generally agree that Christians are vulnerable to the enemy's temptation, accusation, and deception. But for some reason we hesitate to admit that Christians can lose their freedom and can surrender to demonic influences. However, the evidence of Scripture is abundant and clear that believers who repeatedly succumb to temptation, accusation, and deception can lose control.

Let me quickly add that demonic *control* does not mean satanic *ownership*. Like Sheila, you have been purchased by the blood of the Lamb, and not even the powers of hell can take your salvation away from you (1 Peter 1:17-19; Romans 8:35-39). In his book *What Demons Can Do to Saints*, Dr. Merrill Unger writes: "The demon enters...as a squatter and not as an owner or a guest or as one who has a right there. But he comes in as an intruder and as an invader and enemy. But come he does if the door is open by serious and protracted sin."[1] Satan knows he can never own you again. But if he can deceive you into yielding control of your life to him in some way, he can neutralize your growth and your impact in the world for Christ.

BETWEEN THE DEMONIAC AND THE APOSTLE

The debate usually centers on the question "Is it possible for a Christian to be demon-possessed?" Many who argue the issue tend to see demon possession as evidenced by the Gadarene demoniac (Luke 8): stark, raving mad from being the habitat of a legion of demons.

Perhaps we should state the question this way: can an evil spirit and the Holy Spirit occupy the same space in a human life? The god of this world occupies a place in our atmosphere, and so does the Holy Spirit. And Satan presently has access to our Father in heaven. So it should not be thought impossible that demonic influence can partially control the life of one in whom the Holy Spirit also dwells. If this possibility is difficult for you to swallow, I encourage you to read *Demon Possession and the Christian*, by C. Fred Dickason.

In New Testament Greek, the term "demon-possessed" doesn't exist. It's only one word—*daimonizomai* (verb) or *daimonizomenos* (participle)—which is best transliterated "demonized" (Matthew 4:24; 9:32; 15:22; Mark 5:15). Another expression of the concept of being demonized is the phrase *echein daimonion*, which means to "have a demon." The religious leaders used this phrase when they accused both John the Baptist and Jesus of being demonized (Luke 7:33; John 7:20).

To be demonized means to be under the control of one or more demons. Demonization is not a matter of extremes, such as the either/or idea of being completely free or totally bound; it's a matter of degrees. Since we live in a world whose god is Satan, the possibility of being tempted, deceived, and accused is continuous. If you allow his schemes to influence you, you can lose control to the degree that you have been deceived.

Demonic Control of the Saints

It is critical that Christians understand their vulnerability to demonic influence. Those who say a demon cannot control an area of a believer's life have left us with only two possible culprits for the problems we face: ourselves or God. If we blame ourselves we feel hopeless because we can't do anything to stop what we're doing. If we blame God our confidence in Him as our benevolent Father is shattered. Either way, we have no chance to gain the victory which the Bible promises us. In reality we are in a winnable war against principalities and powers from the defeated kingdom of darkness. But their lies can gain a measure of control if we let them.

Here are several indications in Scripture that believers can lose control or come under bondage.

Luke 13:10-18. While Jesus was teaching in the synagogue, "there was a woman who for eighteen years had had a sickness caused by a spirit; and she was bent double, and could not straighten up at all" (verse 11). Verse 16 states that her physical disability was caused by satanic bondage. This woman was not an unbeliever. She was "a daughter of Abraham" (verse 16), a God-fearing woman of faith with a spiritual problem. As soon as Jesus released her from bondage, her physical problem was cured.

Notice that this woman wasn't protected from demonic control by being inside the synagogue. Neither the walls of a synagogue nor the walls of a church provide a sanctuary from demonic influence. If plaster walls are not a barrier to Satan, do you think your skin is? The spiritual world is not subject to such natural barriers, nor is it limited by the laws of physics.

Admittedly, this event occurred before the cross. But it is an indication that believers are subject to demon control.

Luke 22:31-34. The apostle Peter is an example of a believer who temporarily lost control to Satan. Jesus said to him, "Simon, Simon, behold, Satan has demanded permission to sift you like wheat" (verse 31). What right did Satan have to make such a demand? Peter had apparently given Satan a foothold through pride when he debated with the disciples about which of them was the greatest (Luke 22:24). Even though Peter wholeheartedly intended to stand by his Master to the death (verse 33), Jesus announced that Peter would deny Him three times (verse 34), which he did. It's encouraging to note, however, that Jesus had already prayed for Peter's successful recovery from the incident (verse 32).

Ephesians 6:10-17. This passage contains Paul's familiar exhortation to believers to "put on the full armor of God, that you may be able to stand firm against the schemes of the devil" (verse 11). What is the purpose of armor? To prevent the enemy's arrows from penetrating the body and injuring the soldier. If it is impossible for Satan's arrows to penetrate us, there would be no need for us to put on the armor. The instructions regarding spiritual armor suggest that it is possible for the enemy to penetrate our lives and gain a measure of control.

James 3:14-16. James indicates that if we yield to jealousy and selfish ambition, we may open ourselves to being controlled by wisdom which is "earthly, natural, demonic" (verse 15). I had a student whose logic regarding Scripture was completely confused. He had been completely orthodox in his faith until he encountered a prostitute who challenged his faith to the core. Then he started coming up with all kinds of new "insights," but nobody could understand them. His arguments sounded like they came from a book by Mary Baker Eddy, and none of the other students agreed with him. To my knowledge he never recovered from his experience with demonic logic.

1 Timothy 4:1-3. Paul wrote, "Some will fall away from the faith, paying attention to deceitful spirits and doctrines of demons" (verse 1). If Satan can deceive your mind, he must be working on the inside, where you are vulnerable to his control. Evidences of control mentioned here are unbiblical practices in the areas of eating habits and marriage (verse 3).

1 Corinthians 5:1-13. This passage contains Paul's instructions concerning a man in the Corinthian church who was living in an incestuous relationship with his father's wife (verse 1). He was a man so deluded by Satan and controlled by immorality that he apparently flaunted his illicit relationship before the whole church. Paul's judgment on the matter was severe: "I have decided to deliver such a one to Satan for the destruction of his flesh, that his spirit may be saved in the day of the Lord Jesus" (verse 5). Paul was ready to allow Satan to have his way with the man for awhile in hopes that he would finally say "I've had enough" and repent.

Some wonder if a person at this level of immorality is really a Christian. But if this man were a non-Christian Paul would not have disciplined him, because the church is only required to discipline those within its membership. This man was a believer (at least Paul treated him like one) who had allowed himself to become trapped in immorality. Paul's hope was that he experience the natural consequences of his sin, repent, and be set free from his bondage.

Ephesians 4:26,27. Paul instructed, "'In your anger do not sin': Do not let the sun go down while you are still angry, and do not give the devil a foothold" (NIV). The word "foothold" literally means a "place." Paul is saying that we may allow the devil a place in our lives if we fail to speak the truth in love and manage our emotions. Anger which turns to bitterness and unforgiveness is an open invitation to demonic control (2 Corinthians 2:10,11).

1 Peter 5:6-9. Peter warned, "Your adversary, the devil, prowls about like a roaring lion, seeking someone to devour" (verse 8). The word "devour" means to consume or to swallow up. It is the same word used in 1 Corinthians 15:54: "Death is swallowed up in victory." To be swallowed up by something certainly conveys the thought of being controlled by it. If believers are not vulnerable to being controlled by Satan, Peter would not need to alert us to the possibility.

The context of Peter's warning suggests two conditions which may predispose a believer to vulnerability. In verse 6 we are encouraged to humble ourselves before the Lord. Perhaps with the painful memory of the consequences of his own self-exaltation in mind, Peter indicates that whenever we resist pride we resist Satan. And verses 7 and 8 suggest that if we don't learn how to cast our anxieties on the Lord, we make ourselves easy prey for Satan.

Acts 5:1-11. This is perhaps the most definitive passage on Satan's ability to control believers. At the close of Acts 4 we discover that members of the young Jerusalem church were voluntarily selling property and giving the proceeds to the apostles for use in ministry. "But a certain man named Ananias, with his wife Sapphira, sold a piece of property, and kept back some of the price for himself, with his wife's full knowledge, and bringing a portion of it, he laid it at the apostles' feet. But Peter said, 'Ananias, why has Satan filled your heart to lie to the Holy Spirit, and to keep back some of the price of the land? ... You have not lied to men, but to God'" (verses 1-4).

The issue was not that Ananias and Sapphira withheld part of the proceeds, but that they lied about it, apparently saying that what they gave was the total amount they received. The consequence of the couple's sin was immediate and sobering: They died on the spot (verses 5,10).

Some who have difficulty with satanic control of believers have argued that Ananias and Sapphira were unbelievers. I don't buy that argument. First, Acts 4:31 states that this event took place within the context of the Christian community, of which Ananias and Sapphira were obviously members. Second, Acts 5:11 records, "And great fear came upon the whole church." If God were judging someone *outside* the church, why would great fear come upon those *within* the church? There was great fear among *believers* because God had dramatically displayed His attitude toward *believers* who live a lie. Third, the severity of the punishment indicates that God was underscoring the importance of truth in the community of believers. Unbelievers lie all the time, and they usually are not as swiftly and thoroughly judged as were Ananias and Sapphira. I believe that God was communicating early in the church's history that our major problem is not communism, drugs, or false religions; it's giving in to Satan's deception.

Ananias' problem was that he had allowed Satan's deception to fill (control) his heart. The word "filled" in Acts 5:3 (*pleroo*) is the same word used in Ephesians 5:18: "Be filled with the Spirit." It is possible for the believer to be filled with satanic deception or filled by the Spirit. To whichever source you yield, by that source you shall be filled and controlled. When you allow Satan to deceive you in any area of your life, you are vulnerable to his control in that area.

RESPONSIBILITY FOR RESISTING CONTROL

Lest we tend to lay the total blame for Ananias and Sapphira's demise on Satan, we must remember that these two believers were willing participants in the lie which led to their deaths. Peter confronted Ananias and Sapphira respectively: "Why is it that you have conceived this deed in your heart?"; "Why is it that you have agreed together to put the Spirit of the Lord to the test?" (Acts 5:4,9). Yes, Satan filled their hearts with deception and exerted a measure of control over them in their misdeed. But he was only able to do so because at some point Ananias and Sapphira opened the door for him.

I never tolerate someone saying, "The devil made me do it." No, he didn't make you do it; *you* did it. Somewhere along the line you chose to give the devil a foothold. He merely took advantage of the opportunity you gave him. You have all the resources and protection you need to live a victorious life in Christ every day. If you're not living it, it's your choice. When you leave a door open for the devil by not resisting temptation, accusation, or deception, he will enter it. And if you continue to allow him access to that area, he will eventually control it. You won't lose your salvation, but you will lose your daily victory.

Many Christians today who cannot control their lives in some area wallow in self-blame instead of acting responsibly to solve the problem. They berate themselves and punish themselves for not having the willpower to break a bad habit, when instead they should be resisting Satan in an area where he has obviously robbed them of control. Anything bad which you cannot stop doing, or anything good which you cannot make yourself do, could be an area of demonic control.

If You're Not Responsible, You Will Lose Control

In Chapter 5 we examined the believer's protection in the face of demonic attack. This protection is not something you can take for granted irrespective of how you behave. God's protection is conditional on your willingness to respond to God's provision.

In Romans 13:14 we are instructed to "put on the Lord Jesus Christ, and make no provision for the flesh in regard to its lusts." But what if we *do* make provision for the flesh by giving Satan an opportunity in our life through sin? Do we have blanket immunity from Satan's invasion? No, that protection is conditional on our responsible participation in God's plan for our protection. Dr. Unger writes: "The Holy Spirit indwelling the believer ungrieved by sin (Ephesians 4:30) and unquenched by disobedience (1 Thessalonians 5:19) most certainly precludes invasion by a demon spirit. But who dares assert that a demon spirit will not invade the life of a believer in which the Holy Spirit has been grieved by serious and persistent sin and quenched by flagrant disobedience?"[2]

James 4:7 admonishes us to "resist the devil and he will flee from you." What if we don't resist him? Is he required to flee from us if we don't take our stand against him? No, if we don't resist him, he doesn't have to go. God's protection in this area is guaranteed, but we must activate that protection by personally resisting Satan.

Ephesians 6:10-17 outlines the armor of God which believers are instructed to put on in order to "stand firm against the schemes of the devil" (verse 11). But if we go into battle without some of our armor, are we impervious to getting wounded? No, if we fail to cover ourselves with the armor God has provided, we are vulnerable in those exposed areas. Again Dr. Unger comments:

> If the Christian fails to use his armor, will he [Satan] stop short of invading the believer's citadel? If he does invade, this is precisely why the believer may become enslaved having been "taken captive by him at his will" (2 Timothy 2:26). The believer is invaded and overrun by the enemy, who, like any invading foe, does not permit the use of weapons of any sort by the citizens of the country overrun. As a result there is no struggle, only enforced submission and subservience.[3]

James 4:1 reveals that the source of our quarrels and conflicts is the pleasures that "wage war in your members." Paul instructed, "Do not let sin reign in your mortal body that you should obey its lusts" (Romans 6:12). The world, the flesh, and the devil are continually at war against the life of the Spirit within us. But what if we don't fight back? Will we still be victorious over the pleasures and lusts which strive to reign over us? No, they will control us if we fail to stem their invasion by resisting Satan.

Choosing truth, living a righteous life, and donning the armor of God is each believer's individual responsibility. I cannot be responsible for you, and you cannot be responsible for me. I can pray for you, encourage you in the faith, and support you, but if you go into the battle without your armor on, you may get hurt. As much as that may be a matter of concern for me, I still cannot make those decisions of responsibility for you. Those choices are yours alone.

At this point you may be lamenting with the apostle Paul, "I am not practicing what I would like to do, but I am doing the very thing I hate" (Romans 7:15). You realize that you have been an unwitting target for Satan's temptation, accusation, deception, and control. You have been irresponsible by not resisting Satan as you should. You wonder, "Am I doomed in my dilemma? I have left the door open for Satan, and he has taken advantage of my spiritual passivity. Can I get him out of the places he has wormed into?"

The answer is a resounding yes! Jesus Christ is the Bondage Breaker. But in order to experience His freedom, we must find the doors we left open through which Satan gained entrance. We must say, "Lord, I confess that I am responsible for giving Satan a foothold in my life, and I renounce the involvement with him which has led to my bondage." I call this process the steps to freedom. Are you ready to be free? Chapter 12 will lead you through the biblical steps to freedom, and then you will be free indeed.

PART THREE

Walk Free!

12

Steps to Freedom in Christ

Freedom in Christ from demonic deception and interference is the inheritance of every believer (Galatians 5:1). The church fathers certainly understood the reality of the spiritual world we live in and attested to the victory that is ours in Christ. Tertullian wrote:

> Mock as you like, but get the demons if you can to join you in your mocking; let them deny that Christ is coming to judge every human soul.... Let them deny that, for their wickedness condemned already, they are kept for that very judgment day, with all their worshipers and their works. Why, all the authority and power we have over them is from our naming the name of Christ, and recalling to their memory the woes with which God threatens them.... Fearing Christ in God, and God in Christ, they become subject to the servants of God and Christ. So at our touch and breathing, overwhelmed by the thought and realization of those judgment fires, they leave at our command the bodies they have entered, unwilling and distressed.[1]

Origen encouraged: "The Christian—the true Christian, I mean—who has submitted to God alone and His Word, will suffer nothing from demons, for He is mightier than demons.... For we despise them, and demons, when despised, can do no harm to those who are under the protection of Him who can alone help all who deserve His aid."[2]

Christ has set you free through His victory over sin and death on the cross. But if you have lost a measure of your freedom because you have failed to stand firm in the faith or you have disobeyed God, it is your responsibility to do whatever is necessary to establish a right relationship with God. Your eternal destiny is not at stake; you are secure in Christ. But your daily victory in Him will be tenuous at best if you fail to do your part in laying hold of your freedom.

Remember: You are not the helpless victim of a tug-of-war between two nearly equal heavenly superpowers. Compared to Satan's limited power, God is completely off the charts in His omnipotence, omnipresence, and omniscience—and you are in Him! Sometimes the reality of sin and the presence of evil may seem more real than the reality and presence of God, but that's part of Satan's deception. He is a defeated foe, and we are in Christ the eternal Victor. That's why we worship God: to keep His divine attributes constantly before us in order to counter Satan's lies. A true knowledge of God and our identity in Christ is the greatest determinant of our mental health. A false concept of God and the misplaced deification of Satan are the greatest contributors to mental illness.

In this chapter I want to present seven specific steps you need to take in order to experience the full freedom and victory that Christ purchased for you on the cross. Don't expect someone else to do for you what you alone must do. If you have lost your freedom, it is because of what you have chosen to believe and do. Consequently, your freedom will be the result of what you now choose to believe, confess, forgive, renounce, and forsake. No one can believe for you. The battle for your mind can only be won as you personally choose truth.

As you go through these steps to freedom, remember that Satan will be defeated only if you confront him verbally. He is under no obligation to obey your thoughts. Only God has complete knowledge of your mind. As you take each step, it is important that you submit to God inwardly and then resist the devil verbally by reading aloud each prayer and statement (James 4:7).

The following steps are nothing more than a fierce moral inventory and a rock-solid commitment to truth. Even if your problems stem from a source other than those covered in these steps, you have nothing to lose by going through them. Many Christian counseling ministries around the world are using these steps to freedom with their clients in addition to any personal therapy required. The worst that can happen is that you will get right with God on these issues.

STEP 1: COUNTERFEIT VERSUS REAL

The first step to freedom in Christ is to renounce your previous or current involvements with satanically inspired occultic practices or false religions. You may have tried many ways in the past for resolving your spiritual problems and finding meaning in life. Any activity or group which denies Jesus Christ, offers guidance through any source other than the absolute authority of the written Word of God, or requires secret initiations must be forsaken. No Christian has any business being part of a group that is not completely open about all they do (1 John 1:5,7). If the leaders of any group demand absolute authority instead of serving the needs of their constituents, do not submit to them.

The early church included in its public declaration of faith, "I renounce you, Satan, and all your works and ways." The Catholic Church, the Eastern Orthodox Church, and many other liturgical churches still require this renunciation as part of confirmation. For some reason it has disappeared from most evangelical churches. You must not only choose the truth but disavow Satan and his lies. There is no middle ground with truth. Jesus said, "He who is not with Me is against Me; and he who does not gather with Me scatters" (Luke 11:23). There are not many paths to God;

there is only one way (John 14:6). Christians are not being narrow-minded when they stand on what God has declared.

In assessing counterfeits to Christianity, no criterion is more important than the Person of Jesus Christ. Paul wrote: "I am afraid, lest as the serpent deceived Eve by his craftiness, your minds should be led astray from the simplicity and purity of devotion to Christ. For if one comes and preaches another [*allos*] Jesus whom we have not preached, or you receive a different [*heteros*] spirit which you have not received, or a different [*heteros*] gospel which you have not accepted, you bear this beautifully" (2 Corinthians 11:3,4). Other religions and cults may talk about Jesus, but they present Him in another way than He is presented in Scripture. They may talk about the same historical Jesus, but not about the Son of God, the Alpha and Omega, and the great I AM. Jesus said, "Unless you believe that I am He, you shall die in your sins" (John 8:24). If you believe in Jesus in any other way than how He is presented in the Bible, you will receive an altogether different spirit from the Holy Spirit and an altogether different gospel from the gospel of grace.

In order to help you assess your previous spiritual experiences, complete the "Non-Christian Spiritual Experience Inventory" found in "Further Help" at the back of this book. The list is not exhaustive, but it will guide you in identifying non-Christian involvements. As you go through this step, pray in the following way:

> Dear heavenly Father, I ask You to reveal to me all the occultic practices, false religions, and false teachers with which I have knowingly or unknowingly been involved.

Write down everything God brings to mind. After you are sure your list is complete, pray the following for each practice, religion, and teacher:

> Lord, I confess that I have participated in _____.
> I ask Your forgiveness, and I renounce _____ as a
> counterfeit to true Christianity.

Don't feel bad if you must confess several categories. Many hurting people like you have been misguided in a world which is filled with cults, false religions, and false teachers. I have dealt with people who have checked up to half the list.

Some hesitate to complete the inventory because they don't believe they actually participated in these activities. But if anyone in your family was involved, you may want to put it on your list of activities to renounce just in case you unknowingly gave Satan a foothold. One young woman I counseled had simply ridden along while her mother visited a psychic, and the daughter walked out with her own spirit guide. A former missionary related to me that, while serving in China, he attended a Buddhist funeral and innocently participated in the ritual by taking off his shoes, which is an act of worship in many Eastern religions. That night demons mocked him while he tried to do his devotions. When he heard my tapes on this subject he renounced his participation in a pagan religion and commanded the evil spirits to leave. They did.

Don't be surprised if you encounter some resistance as you complete this step. A Mormon woman who attended one of my conferences told me that an inner voice kept urging her all day, "Get out of here. He is the one I was warning you about." She stayed, however, and found her freedom in Christ. Later she brought other members of her family to another conference. Satan doesn't want you to be free, and he will do whatever he can to keep you from completing these steps to freedom.

STEP 2: DECEPTION VERSUS TRUTH

Truth is primarily the revelation of God's Word, but it

also includes truth in the inner self (Psalm 51:6). When David lived a lie he suffered greatly. When he finally found freedom by acknowledging the truth, he wrote, "How blessed is the man...in whose spirit there is no deceit" (Psalm 32:2). We are to lay aside falsehood and speak the truth in love (Ephesians 4:15,25). A mentally healthy person is one who is in touch with reality and relatively free of anxiety. Both qualities should epitomize the Christian who renounces deception and embraces the truth.

Begin this critical step by expressing aloud the following prayer:

> Dear heavenly Father, I know that You desire truth in the inner self and that facing this truth is the way of liberation (John 8:32). I acknowledge that I have been deceived by the father of lies (John 8:44) and that I have deceived myself (1 John 1:8). I pray in the name of the Lord Jesus Christ that You, heavenly Father, will rebuke all deceiving spirits by virtue of the shed blood and resurrection of the Lord Jesus Christ. And since by faith I have received You into my life and am now seated with Christ in the heavenlies (Ephesians 2:6), I command all deceiving spirits to depart from me. I now ask the Holy Spirit to guide me into all truth (John 16:13). I ask You to "search me, O God, and know my heart; try me and know my anxious thoughts; and see if there be any hurtful way in me, and lead me in the everlasting way" (Psalm 139:23,24).
>
> In Jesus' name I pray. Amen.

Choosing the truth may be difficult if you have been living a lie for many years. You may need to seek professional help to weed out the defense mechanisms you have depended upon all this time to survive. The Christian needs only one defense: Jesus. Knowing that you are forgiven and accepted as God's child sets you free to face reality and declare your dependence on Him.

Deception is the most subtle of all satanic strongholds. Have you ever noticed that all people with addictive behavior lie to themselves and others almost continuously? The alcoholic lies about his drinking, the anorexic lies about her eating, and the sex offender lies about his behavior. Lying is an evil defense prompted by the father of lies, Satan (John 8:44). One pastor told me about a group of recovering alcoholics in his church who were forming a support group. They insisted that the slogan on their brochure read: "Are you tired of listening to those voices?" Attend an AA meeting and you will hear phrases such as "Don't pay attention to the committee in your head." Satan's lies are at the heart of addictive behavior. The spiritual side of addictive behavior cannot be overlooked.

Faith is the biblical response to the truth, and believing the truth is a choice. When someone says, "I want to believe God, but I just can't," he or she is being deceived. Of course you can believe God! Faith is something you *decide to do*, not something you *feel like doing*. Believing the truth doesn't make it true; it's true, so we believe it. The New Age movement and the "name it and claim it" adherents are distorting the truth by saying that we create reality through what we believe. Faith doesn't *create* reality; faith *responds to* reality. It's not the idea that you merely "believe" that counts; it's what or who you *believe in* that counts. Everybody believes in something, and everybody walks by faith according to what he or she believes. But if what you believe isn't true, then how you live won't be right.

Your faith is only as great as your knowledge of the object of your faith. If you have little knowledge of God and His Word, you will have little faith. That's why faith can't be pumped up. Any attempt to live by faith beyond what you absolutely know to be true is presumption. If you only believe what you feel, you will be led through life by one emotional impulse after another. The path of truth begins with the truth of God's Word. Believe the truth and walk by faith according to what you believe, and then your feelings will line up with what you think and how you behave.

Historically the church has found great value in publicly declaring its beliefs. The Apostles' Creed and the Nicene Creed have been recited for centuries. Read aloud the following affirmation of faith, and do so again as often as necessary to renew your mind and take your stand according to the truth. I recommend that you read it daily for several weeks, especially if you are just resolving a personal spiritual conflict.

Doctrinal Affirmation

I recognize that there is only one true and living God (Exodus 20:2,3), who exists as the Father, Son, and Holy Spirit, and that He is worthy of all honor, praise, and worship as the Creator, Sustainer, and Beginning and End of all things (Revelation 4:11; 5:9,10; Isaiah 43:1,7,21).

I recognize Jesus Christ as the Messiah, the Word who became flesh and dwelt among us (John 1:1,14). I believe that He came to destroy the works of Satan (1 John 3:8), that He disarmed the rulers and authorities and made a public display of them, having triumphed over them (Colossians 2:15).

I believe that God has proven His love for me, because when I was still a sinner Christ died for me (Romans 5:8). I believe that He delivered me from the domain of darkness and transferred me to His kingdom, and in Him I have redemption, the forgiveness of sins (Colossians 1:13,14).

I believe that I am now a child of God (1 John 3:1-3), and that I am seated with Christ in the heavenlies (Ephesians 2:6). I believe that I was saved by the grace of God through faith, that it was a gift and not the result of any works on my part (Ephesians 2:8).

I choose to be strong in the Lord and in the strength of His might (Ephesians 6:10). I put no confidence in the flesh (Philippians 3:3), for the weapons of my warfare are not of the flesh (2 Corinthians 10:4). I put on the whole armor of God (Ephesians 6:10-17), and I resolve to stand firm in my faith and resist the evil one

I believe that Jesus has all authority in heaven and on earth (Matthew 28:18), and that He is the head over all rule and authority (Colossians 2:10). I believe that Satan and his demons are subject to me in Christ because I am a member of Christ's body (Ephesians 1:19-23). I therefore obey the command to resist the devil (James 4:7), and I command him in the name of Christ to leave my presence

I believe that apart from Christ I can do nothing (John 15:5), so I declare my dependence on Him. I choose to abide in Christ in order to bear much fruit and glorify the Lord (John 15:8). I announce to Satan that Jesus is my Lord (1 Corinthians 12:3), and I reject any counterfeit gifts or works of Satan in my life

I believe that the truth will set me free (John 8:32), and that walking in the light is the only path of fellowship (1 John 1:7). Therefore, I stand against Satan's deception by taking every thought captive in obedience to Christ (2 Corinthians 10:5). I declare that the Bible is the only authoritative standard (2 Timothy 3:15-17) I choose to speak the truth in love (Ephesians 4:15).

I choose to present my body as an instrument of righteousness, a living and holy sacrifice, and I renew my mind by the living Word of God in order that I may prove that the will of God is good, acceptable, and perfect (Romans 6:13; 12:1,2).

I ask my heavenly Father to fill me with His Holy Spirit (Ephesians 5:18), to lead me into all truth (John 16:13), and to empower my life so that I may live above sin and not carry out the desires of the flesh (Galatians 5:16). I crucify the flesh (Galatians 5:24) and choose to walk by the Spirit.

I renounce all selfish goals and choose the ultimate goal of love (1 Timothy 1:5). I choose to obey the greatest commandment, to love the Lord my God with all my heart, soul, and mind, and to love my neighbor as myself (Matthew 22:37-39).

STEP 3: BITTERNESS VERSUS FORGIVENESS

Most of the ground that Satan gains in the lives of Christians is due to unforgiveness. We are warned to forgive others so that Satan cannot take advantage of us (2 Corinthians 2:10,11). God requires us to forgive others from our hearts or He will turn us over to the tormentors (Matthew 18:34,35). Why is forgiveness so critical to our freedom? Because of the cross. God didn't give us what we *deserve*; He gave us what we *needed* according to His mercy. We are to be merciful just as our heavenly Father is merciful (Luke 6:36). We are to forgive as we have been forgiven (Ephesians 4:31,32).

Forgiveness is not forgetting. People who try to forget find that they cannot. God says He will "remember no more" our sins (Hebrews 10:17), but God, being omniscient, cannot forget. "Remember no more" means that God will never use the past against us (Psalm 103:12). Forgetting may be a result of forgiveness, but it is never the means of forgiveness. When we bring up the past against others, we haven't forgiven them.

Forgiveness is a choice, a crisis of the will. Since God requires us to forgive, it is something we can do. (He would never require us to do something we cannot do.) But forgiveness is difficult for us because it pulls against our concept of justice. We want revenge for offenses suffered. But we are told never to take our own revenge (Romans 12:19). "Why should I let them off the hook?" we protest. You let them off *your* hook, but they are never off God's hook. He will deal with them fairly—something we cannot do.

If you don't let offenders off your hook, you are hooked to them and the past, and that just means continued pain for you. Stop the pain; let it go. You don't forgive someone merely for their sake; you do it for *your* sake so you can be free. Your need to forgive isn't an issue between you and the offender; it's between you and God.

Forgiveness is agreeing to live with the consequences of another person's sin. Forgiveness is costly; we pay the price of the evil we forgive. Yet you're going to live with those consequences whether you want to or not; your only choice is whether you will do so in the bitterness of unforgiveness or the freedom of forgiveness. That's how Jesus forgave you—He took the consequences of your sin upon Himself. All true forgiveness is substitutional, because no one really forgives without bearing the penalty of the other person's sin.

Why then do we forgive? Because Christ forgave us. God the Father "made Him who knew no sin to be sin on our behalf, that we might become the righteousness of God in Him" (2 Corinthians 5:21). Where is the justice? The cross makes forgiveness legally and morally right: "For the death that He died, He died to sin, once for all" (Romans 6:10).

How do you forgive from the heart? First you acknowledge the hurt and the hate. If your forgiveness doesn't visit the emotional core of your past, it will be incomplete. This is the great evangelical cover-up. Christians feel the pain of interpersonal offenses, but we won't acknowledge it. Let God bring the pain to the surface so He can deal with it. This is where the healing takes place. Ask God to bring to your mind those you need to forgive as you read the following prayer aloud:

> Dear heavenly Father, I thank You for the riches of Your kindness, forbearance, and patience, knowing that Your kindness has led me to repentance (Romans 2:4). I confess that I have not extended that same patience and kindness toward others who have offended me, but instead I have harbored bitterness and resentment. I pray that during this time of self-examination You would bring to mind only those people that I have not forgiven in order that I may do so (Matthew 18:35). I also pray that if I have offended others You would bring to mind only those people from whom I need to seek forgiveness and the extent to which I need to seek it (Matthew 5:23,24). I ask this in the precious name of Jesus. Amen.

As you pray, be prepared to have names come to your mind that have been blocked from your memory. In 95 percent of the people I work with in this process, the first two names which come to mind are their parents. The other often overlooked name on the list is self. Why might you need to forgive yourself? Because when you discovered that you can't blame God for your problems, you blamed yourself.

Make a list of all those who have offended you. Face the cross; it makes forgiveness legally and morally right. Since God has forgiven them, you can too. Decide that you will bear the burden of their offenses by not using the information about their offenses against them in the future. This doesn't mean that you tolerate their sin. Tolerating sin makes a mockery of forgiveness. You must always take a stand against sin.

Don't wait to forgive until you feel like forgiving; you will never get there. Feelings take time to heal after the choice to forgive is made and Satan has lost his place (Ephesians 4:26,27).

For each person on your list, say: "Lord, I forgive (name) for (offenses)." Don't say, "Lord, please help me to forgive," because He is already helping you. Don't say, "Lord, I want to forgive," because you are bypassing the hard-core choice to forgive, which is your own personal responsibility. Keep praying about each individual until you are sure that all the remembered pain has been dealt with. As you pray, God may bring to mind offending people and experiences you have totally forgotten. Let Him do it even if it is painful for you. He wants you to be free. I have seen many people forgive unspeakable atrocities with a great deal of emotion, but the freedom which resulted was tremendous. Don't try to rationalize or explain the offender's behavior. Forgiveness deals with your pain, not another's behavior. Remember: Positive feelings will follow in time; freeing yourself from the past is the critical issue.

STEP 4: REBELLION VERSUS SUBMISSION

We live in a rebellious generation of individuals who feel it is their right to sit in judgment of those in authority over them. Christians are no exception. Church members critique the choir and criticize the sermon. We would be far better off if we entered into worship instead of critiquing it and allowed the sermon to judge us instead of criticizing it.

Rebelling against God leads to nothing but trouble. As our commanding general, the Lord says, "Get into ranks and follow me. I will not lead you into temptation, and I will deliver you from evil." But we sometimes say, "No, I don't want to follow today." So we fall out of ranks, do our own thing, and get shot. Then we blame God for not protecting us.

We are also tempted to rebel against human authority. We have two biblical responsibilities in regard to authority figures: pray for them and submit to them. The only time God permits us to disobey earthly leaders is when they require us to do something morally wrong before God. Study the following passages of Scripture to further understand our response to authority: civil government (Romans 13:1-5; 1 Timothy 2:1-4; 1 Peter 2:13-16); parents (Ephesians 6:1-3); husband (1 Peter 3:1,2); employer (1 Peter 2:18-21); church leaders (Hebrews 13:17).

Being submissive to human authority demonstrates faith. As you submit to God's line of authority, you are choosing to believe that God will protect you and bless you, and that all will go well with you. Ask God to forgive you for those times you have not been submissive, and declare your trust in God to work through His established lines of authority. After you have confessed any willful rebellion to God, pray the following prayer aloud:

> Dear heavenly Father, You have said that rebellion is as the sin of witchcraft and insubordination is as iniquity and idolatry (1 Samuel 15:23). I know that in action and attitude I have sinned against You with a rebellious heart. I ask Your forgiveness for my rebellion and pray that by the shed blood of the Lord Jesus Christ all ground gained by evil spirits because of my rebelliousness would be canceled. I pray that You will shed light on all my ways that I may know the full extent of my rebelliousness and choose to adopt a submissive spirit and a servant's heart. In the name of Christ Jesus my Lord. Amen.

STEP 5: PRIDE VERSUS HUMILITY

Pride is a killer. Pride says, "I can do it alone. I can get myself out of this mess without God's help." Oh, no you can't! We absolutely need God, and we desperately need each other. Paul wrote, "We are the true circumcision, who worship in the Spirit of God and glory in Christ Jesus and put no confidence in the flesh" (Philippians 3:3). Humility is confidence properly placed. Examine the instructions on pride and humility in James 4:6-10 and 1 Peter 5:1-10. The context reveals that spiritual conflict follows the expression of pride. Pride is what caused Lucifer to be thrown out of heaven. Use the following prayer to express your commitment to live humbly before God:

> Dear heavenly Father, You have said that pride goes before destruction and an arrogant spirit before stumbling (Proverbs 16:18). I confess that I have not denied myself, picked up my cross daily, and followed You (Matthew 16:24). In so doing I have given ground to the enemy in my life. I have believed that I could be successful and live victoriously by my own strength and resources. I now confess that I have sinned against You by placing my will before Yours and by centering my life around self instead of You. I now renounce the self life and by so doing cancel all the ground that has been gained in my members by the enemies of the Lord Jesus Christ. I pray that You will guide me so that I will do nothing from selfishness or empty conceit, but that with humility of mind I will regard others as more important than myself (Philippians 2:3). Enable me through love to serve others and in honor prefer others (Romans 12:10). I ask this in the name of Christ Jesus my Lord. Amen.

STEP 6: BONDAGE VERSUS FREEDOM

The next step to freedom deals with habitual sin. People who have been caught in the trap of sin-confess-sin-confess may need to follow the instructions of James 5:16: "Confess your sins to one another, and pray for one another, so that you may be healed. The effective prayer of a righteous man can accomplish much." Seek out a righteous person who will hold you up in prayer and to whom you can be accountable. Others may need only the assurance of 1 John 1:9: "If we confess our sins, He is faithful and righteous to forgive us our sins and to cleanse us from all unrighteousness."

Whether you need the help of others or just the accountability of God, pray the following prayer:

> Dear heavenly Father, You have told us to put on the Lord Jesus Christ and make no provision for the flesh in regard to its lusts (Romans 13:14). I acknowledge that I have given in to fleshly lusts which wage war against my soul (1 Peter 2:11). I thank You that in Christ my sins are forgiven, but I have transgressed Your holy law and given the enemy an opportunity to wage war in my members (Ephesians 4:27; James 4:1; 1 Peter 5:8). I come before Your presence to acknowledge these sins and to seek Your cleansing (1 John 1:9) that I may be freed from the bondage of sin (Galatians 5:1). I now ask You to reveal to my mind the ways that I have transgressed Your moral law and grieved the Holy Spirit.

After you have confessed all known sin, pray:

> I now confess these sins to You and claim through
> the blood of the Lord Jesus Christ my forgiveness
> and cleansing. I cancel all ground that evil spirits
> have gained through my willful involvement in sin.
> I ask this in the wonderful name of my Lord and
> Savior Jesus Christ. Amen.

STEP 7: ACQUIESCENCE VERSUS RENUNCIATION

The last step to freedom is to renounce the sins of your
ancestors and any curses which may have been placed on
you. In giving the Ten Commandments, God said: "You
shall not make for yourself an idol, or any likeness of what is
in heaven above or on the earth beneath or in the water
under the earth. You shall not worship them or serve them;
for I, the Lord your God, am a jealous God, visiting the
iniquity of the fathers on the children, on the third and
fourth generations of those who hate Me" (Exodus 20:4,5).
The fact that demonic strongholds can be passed on from
one generation to the next is well-attested by those who
counsel the afflicted. This is not to deny that many problems are transmitted genetically or acquired from an immoral atmosphere. All three conditions can predispose an
individual to a particular sin.

When you tear down a satanic stronghold which has been
established in your family, expect resistance. One of my
seminary students sat stunned after praying through this
seventh step. "I can't believe it," he exclaimed. "I had to
hang onto my chair to keep from running out of the room
during that last prayer."

"What's your family heritage?" I asked.

"My mother is a psychic, totally into New Age!"

The devil doesn't want to give up his territory and will try
to interrupt you when you take authority over him.

An ex-Mormon woman was praying through this step

when she suddenly stopped in panic. "Tell me what you hear," I asked.

"You mean you don't see him there?"

"Who?"

"My dead father—standing right there behind you."

I didn't look around because what she was seeing was in her mind, and it wasn't her father.

"What's with your father?" I asked.

"I'm responsible for him," she said. Mormons believe that they are responsible for family members. They will even marry and be baptized for dead relatives. When this woman renounced her relationship with that spirit and her Mormon beliefs, she was free from the demonic hold.

Mormons have their own subtle form of ancestor worship. One of my students was asked to help a Mormon girlfriend who was under tremendous spiritual attack. The girlfriend's parents went on a trip to Salt Lake City to study their genealogy. They prayed that the spirits of their dead ancestors would protect their daughter while they were gone. The demons took advantage of the invitation and terrorized the girl. When my student led her to Christ she was free of the attack.

Adopted children can be especially subject to demonic strongholds because of their natural parentage. But even an adopted child can become a new creation in Christ, and must actively renounce old strongholds and embrace his or her inheritance as God's child.

If you have been subject to satanic ritual there is a good chance that you were assigned a spiritual "guardian" or "parent." These spiritual relationships must be specifically renounced along with any blood pacts uniting you to anyone but God. I was getting nowhere with a victim of satanic abuse until she told me that, in one ritual, a brown-haired lady was assigned to be her mother. When she renounced that relationship she was free to process the rest of her problems. If you are the victim of ritual abuse, seek the help of a skilled counselor who understands demonic strongholds.

In order to walk free from past influences, pray the following prayer:

> Dear heavenly Father, I come to You as Your child, purchased by the blood of the Lord Jesus Christ. I here and now reject and disown all the sins of my ancestors. As one who has been delivered from the power of darkness and translated into the kingdom of God's dear Son, I cancel out all demonic working that has been passed on to me from my ancestors. As one who has been crucified and raised with Christ and who sits with Him in heavenly places, I reject any and every way in which Satan may claim ownership of me. I declare myself to be eternally and completely signed over and committed to the Lord Jesus Christ. I now command every familiar spirit and every enemy of the Lord Jesus Christ that is in or around me to flee my presence and never to return. I now ask You, heavenly Father, to fill me with Your Holy Spirit. I submit my body as an instrument of righteousness, a living sacrifice, that I may glorify You in my body. All this I do in the name and authority of the Lord Jesus Christ. Amen.

Once you have secured your freedom by going through these seven steps, you may find demonic influences attempting reentry days or even months later. One person told me that she heard a spirit say to her mind "I'm back" two days after she had been set free. "No, you're not," she proclaimed aloud. The attack ceased immediately.

One victory does not constitute winning the war. But many victories are the mark of a successful warrior. Freedom must be maintained. One jubilant lady asked after completing these steps, "Will I always be like this?" I told her that she would stay free as long as she remained in right relationship with God. "Even if you slip and fall," I encouraged, "you know how to get right with God again."

One victim of incredible atrocities shared with me an excellent illustration, after finding her freedom in Christ. In her illustration, she was forced to play a game with an ugly stranger in her own home. She kept losing the game and wanted to quit, but the ugly stranger wouldn't let her. Finally she called the police (a higher authority), and they came and escorted the stranger out. When he knocked on the door trying to regain entrance, she recognized his voice and didn't let him in.

What a beautiful illustration of our freedom in Christ. We call upon Christ and He escorts the enemy out of our lives. But it's our responsibility not to let him back in (Galatians 5:1). Stand firm and resist him. This is a winnable war!

Helping Others Find Freedom in Christ

"Are you an exorcist?" a lady once asked after hearing me tell about some of the people I have helped find freedom from demonic influence.

"No, I'm not an exorcist," I replied. "I don't think there is such a thing as an exorcist or that there is a gift of exorcism."

Over the years I have been privileged to see God se hundreds of people free from spiritual bondage througl my ministry. Consequently, many people like the lady above think I have some special gift in this area. I don't. I believe that every committed Christian, especially pastors and counselors, can do what I do to help others find freedom in Christ. Helping others to freedom does not require the exercise of a a special gift; it merely requires the application of truth. Gifts and unique callings are not transferable, but the truth is.

I have trained hundreds of Christians—students, homemakers, pastors, missionaries, laymen—in how to help others find their freedom in Christ. In this chapter I want to summarize the procedure for using the steps to freedom described in the previous chapter. Whether you are a "professional" helper, such as a pastor or counselor, or just a committed Christian who is willing to be used by God to help others, these pages will give you some practical guidelines for successful ministry.

Misconceptions about Helping People in Bondage

Satan's first and foremost strategy is *deception*. The fact that every pastor and counselor has been deceived by the enemy at one time or another in his or her ministry to demonized people is a given. I certainly have been and will be again. As long as Satan's influence in a person's life remains undetected, he is content to lie low and not show his hand. Like a snake in the grass, he quietly sneaks up on his prey and squeezes the life out of it.

But when you confront Satan's deception and expose his lies with the truth, his strategy changes from stealth to power. He becomes the roaring lion that Peter warned about (1 Peter 5:8). The procedure that most Christian counselors follow in dealing with people in whom demonic strongholds have been exposed is to challenge the spirit to manifest itself, and then to cast it out. The helper may feel it necessary to command the spirit to give its name or otherwise identify itself. Inevitably there is a power struggle which provokes the victim to either lapse into a catatonic state, become generally disoriented, or run out of the room. I've seen people get physically injured during such confrontations. This procedure can potentially create more harm than help, especially for the novice.

I have four concerns about this procedure for helping others find freedom in Christ. I encourage you to consider these if you want to help people and avoid playing into the enemy's hand.

1. *We have mistakenly formulated our methods for dealing with demonic powers from the Gospels instead of the epistles.* This is easy to do, since the only specific examples of demonic expulsion are found in Matthew, Mark, Luke, John, and Acts. But the Gospels are the historical record of events which occurred prior to the cross. All authority had not yet been given "in heaven and on earth" (Matthew 28:18). Satan had not yet been defeated at the cross, disarmed, and exposed (Colossians 2:15). During this period a special agent with heaven-sent authority was needed to demonstrate the presence of God.

Some Christians object to making such a sharp distinction between the Gospels and the epistles. Yet all dispensational as well as covenantal theologians see at least some distinctions in moving from law to grace and from the old covenant to the new covenant. For example, if a wealthy leader in your community asked you what he must do to have eternal life, would you tell him to keep the commandments, as Jesus instructed the rich young ruler (Matthew 19:16,17)? Before the cross and under the law you would call him to the righteous standards of the law. But after the cross and under grace you would proclaim the gospel to him. Obviously our approach to evangelism changed after Pentecost. Shouldn't our approach to dealing with issues of freedom change as well?

The Book of Acts is the historical account of the period of transition between the cross and the completion of the canon of Scripture. There is a great deal of disagreement among Christians about how much method and theology we should extract from this important book. Therefore I stress caution in translating examples of demonic expulsion from Acts into doctrinal absolutes. Form follows function, but hosts of problems arise when we define function from form. The Book of Acts helps us realize that satanic encounters continued after the cross and that evil forces continue to exist in opposition to the growth of the church. But this historical book does not constitute the final word on dealing with those forces.

2. *Some have mistakenly argued that no continuing ministry of setting captives free exists in the church because the epistles contain no specific instructions for it.* But there *are* instructions throughout the epistles when you realize that the ultimate responsibility for spiritual freedom belongs to the individual believer, not an outside agent. It's not what you do as the counselor that counts; it's what the counselee believes, confesses, renounces, forgives, etc. You cannot take the steps to freedom for anyone but yourself. All you

can do for others is guide them through the steps to freedom which they must take themselves. If you are successful
in casting a demon out of someone without his or her
involvement, what is to keep it from coming back when you
leave? Unless the individual takes responsibility for his own
freedom, he may end up like the poor fellow who was freed
from one spirit only to be occupied by seven others who
were worse than the first (Matthew 12:43-45).

Many of my colleagues still prefer to confront demons
head-on. They have their stories of success, but readily
admit that when the encounter was unsuccessful it was
because the individual was unwilling to get right with
God. If you feel comfortable and are finding success in a
confrontational procedure, God bless you. But I always
caution those who deal directly with demons not to believe
anything they say. They are all liars (John 8:44). Some
suggest asking the spirit, "Will your confession stand as
truth before the throne of God?" This may work, but I find
no assurance in Scripture that it will.

I have not attempted to "cast out a demon" in several
years. But I have seen hundreds of people find freedom in
Christ as I helped them resolve their personal and spiritual
conflicts. I no longer deal directly with demons at all, and I
prohibit their manifestation. I only work with their victims.
As helpers, our success is dependent upon the cooperation
of the persons we help. We say with Jesus to those we help,
"Be it done to you according to your faith" (Matthew 9:29).
Helping people understand the truth and assume personal
responsibility for truth in their life is the essence of ministry.

3. *We have mistakenly regarded freedom as the product of a
power encounter instead of a truth encounter.* We must avoid
buying into Satan's second strategy of power as much as we
avoid swallowing his first strategy of deception. It isn't
power per se that sets the captive free; it's *truth* (John 8:32).
The power of the Christian is in the truth; the power of

Satan is in the lie. To the satanist, power is everything, but power is only effective in the darkness. The Christian is to pursue the truth because power and authority are already inherent in him. Truth is what makes an encounter with Satan effective. Satan's demonstration of power (which is also deceptive because his power has actually been broken by the cross) is intended to provoke a fear response. When fear is controlling a believer, the Spirit of God is not, and Satan has the upper hand. Fear of the enemy and faith in God are mutually exclusive.

Satan fears detection more than anything else. Whenever the light of truth comes on, he and his demons, like cockroaches, head for the shadows. I have had people tell me that the demons in them are afraid of me. If you are a counselor, don't let a statement like that go to your head. They are really afraid of being detected by and exposed to the *truth*. I have also had people tell me that the demons in them are laughing at me in mockery. This is just another strategy of intimidation designed to put us on the defensive as counselors. As soon as you expose the strategy, the mocking stops.

I will do everything I can to prevent Satan from manifesting himself and glorifying himself through a power encounter. We are to glorify *God* by allowing *His* presence to be manifested in our encounters with demons.

4. *We have wrongly assumed that the main qualification for helping others find freedom is an unusual giftedness or calling instead of character and the ability to teach.* The instructions in the epistles for helping others find freedom in Christ are best summarized in 2 Timothy 2:24-26: "The Lord's bond-servant must not be quarrelsome, but be kind to all, able to teach, patient when wronged, with gentleness correcting those who are in opposition, if perhaps God may grant them repentance leading to the knowledge of the truth, and they may come to their senses and escape the snare of the devil, having been held captive by him to do his will."

This is not a power model; this is a truth model. It requires that the Lord's bondservant be mature in character as expressed by love for people and evidenced by the fruit of the Spirit. It is also important that we are able to communicate the truth so the captive can be set free.

Focusing on character and teaching will keep the counselor from polarizing into a psychotherapeutic procedure which ignores the reality of the spiritual world, or into a deliverance ministry which ignores the whole person. Freedom is transferable because it doesn't depend on any unusual gifts or calling, but on faith, hope, and love. Freedom lasts because, as in any counseling procedure, if the counselee makes the decisions and assumes personal responsibility, the results are far better than if the counselor attempts to do it all.

Furthermore, this passage requires that we be absolutely dependent on God, because He alone can grant repentance and set the captive free. I always start any attempt at helping others by declaring my total dependence on God my Father.

GUIDELINES FOR HELPING PEOPLE FIND FREEDOM

Let me suggest to you a counseling procedure for dealing with people in bondage. It's not the only way to do it, but hundreds of people I have trained have found it to be a workable program for walking others through the steps to freedom.

The normal skills employed in counseling apply to this procedure. You must be compassionate, nonjudgmental, and understanding. You must be more willing to listen than to respond. Solomon warned, "He who gives an answer before he hears, it is folly and shame to him" (Proverbs 18:13).

Another vital requirement for being a helper is that you believe the person you're trying to help. There are countless numbers of people around you who desperately need your help, but they won't come to you if they suspect that you won't believe what they tell you about themselves or their experiences. Nearly every person I have counseled has been counseled by someone else—sometimes for months or years. Most of these people relate to me experiences and thoughts that they haven't revealed to other counselors. It's not my skills as a counselor that opens them up, but their confidence that I believe them.

1. Gather Background Information

I start by learning as much about the person as I can. If possible, I have them fill out a Non-Christian Spiritual Experience Inventory and a Confidential Personal Inventory (see "Further Help" at the back of this book) before our first visit. You may want to use these forms, or adaptations of them, in your counseling.

One reason I want background information on the counselee's family and personal life is to determine if his or her problem is the result of spiritual or natural causes. For example, people with glandular problems often exhibit many of the same emotional problems displayed by someone under demonic attack. Often physical problems such as low blood sugar lead to emotional problems, which in turn open the door for demonic activity. A counselor and a godly medical doctor working together are a good combination. Satan doesn't play fair; he feasts on people who are weak or ill.

First I want to know about the counselee's family history. Were his parents or grandparents involved in the occult or a counterfeit religion? Was there harmony in the home? Are there any divorces or affairs in the family history? Most false beliefs are formed during the developmental years of childhood. For example, many children wrongly blame themselves for their parents' divorce. Others harbor bitterness toward their parents for years because of something which happened in the home. Exposing these false beliefs is integral to helping them find the counselee find freedom.

Was incest or adultery present? Were there any addictive problems, such as alcoholism or drug abuse? Is there a history of mental illness? What type of exercise and eating habits characterized the family? What was the moral climate in the home? Typically, either legalism or license in the extreme leads to later problems.

Next I want to know about the individual counselee. Remember: Don't try to separate the spiritual from the mental and emotional. You must deal with the *whole person*. Therefore you need to know what's going on in all sectors of the counselee's life.

At the physical level, I want to know what his or her eating habits are like, if he has any addictions, if he is under medication, or if he has trouble sleeping. I want to know if he is adopted or has ever been molested.

In the mental area, I want to know if he or she is struggling with obsessive thoughts or if he ever hears "voices." I often ask if he has any foul thoughts about God, especially in church or during devotions. Thoughts of suicide are almost a given for those with major spiritual conflicts. I also need to know what he is putting into his mind by way of reading material, movies, or TV, and if he has any kind of devotional life with God through prayer and Bible study.

At the emotional level, I want to know how much fear he experiences and what he is afraid of (if he knows). Fear is a given for those under demonic attack.

Finally, I want to know about his or her spiritual life. Does he have assurance of his salvation? Many people I counsel believe they have committed the unpardonable sin and have lost their salvation. When Satan deceives Christians into doubting their salvation, they will cease to stand firm in Christ and rely on God. Nothing is more defeating to believers caught in spiritual conflict than to have well-meaning friends say, "Real Christians don't have this kind of problem, so you must not be saved." It's a lie of Satan sent to destroy them.

2. Confront False Concepts

Once I have heard the counselee's story, I try to determine what he or she believes about God and themselves. I have a complete set of professionally produced audio and video tapes which presents who we are in Christ, how to walk by faith, the nature of the spiritual battle for the mind, how to handle emotions and resolve emotional problems from the past, and how to forgive others. The tapes also teach the authority and protection of the believer in spiritual warfare. These taped sessions confront false beliefs about God and self with biblical truth. If possible, I have each counselee go through a set of tapes before we meet. This saves me a lot of time in the counseling sessions, especially when the counselee can review tapes at home several times. I suggest that you purchase a set of tapes or prepare a set of your own tapes which cover the basics of the believer's relationship with God.

Most people in spiritual conflict have a distorted concept of God. Mentally they may have embraced correct theology, but emotionally they embrace something different. Notice in Figure 13a how true concepts of God are filtered through a grid of negative experiences to produce false concepts of God. These false concepts must be replaced by truth in order for freedom to be realized.

A pastor's wife who came to me for counseling told me about her rigidly moral home which was dominated by her demanding mother. The father was a wimp who knew better than to interrupt the mother's tirades against their daughter.

"You really love Jesus, don't you?" I asked the pastor's wife.

"Oh, yes," she responded.

"And you really love the Holy Spirit."

"Yes, I do."

"But you don't even like God the Father, do you?"

Loving and caring → → Hateful and unconcerned

Good and merciful → → Mean and unforgiving

Unconditional grace → → Conditional approval

Present and available → → Absent when needed

Giver of good gifts → → Takes away, "killjoy"

Nurturing and affirming → → Critical and unpleasable

Accepting → → Rejecting

Just, fair, and impartial → → Unjust, unfair, partial

Steadfast and reliable → → Unpredictable and untrust-worthy

Truth about God is filtered through the grid of:

1. Ignorance

2. False prophets and teachers

3. Blasphemous mental thoughts

4. Unhealthy interpersonal relationships during early developmental years

5. Role model of authority figures, especially parents

Figure 13a

She could only respond with tears. Her concept of the heavenly Father was distorted by the image of her earthly father. She perceived Jesus and the Holy Spirit as actively involved with her, but in her mind God the Father, like her earthly father, just sat around passive and uncaring while she went through torture in her life.

I often ask, "If you performed better, would God love you more?" Most people know the right answer: no. But when I ask if they feel loved by God, most express that they show more love and concern for their own children than they expect God to show for them (see Luke 11:9-13). This is all part of Satan's strategy to raise up thoughts against the knowledge of God (2 Corinthians 10:5). If the enemy can keep people from a true concept of God, he can destroy their hope in God.

False self-concepts are very common in people under demonic attack. Many will state that they are different, that the Christian life won't work for them as it does for others, and that they are not entitled to claim God's promises. Many of those in spiritual conflict fear a mental breakdown and are filled with anxiety. Almost all feel unloved, worthless, and rejected. They have tried everything they can think of to improve their self-image, but nothing works. Most of these suspect that their problem is spiritual in nature, but they have no one to turn to. The subject of demonic influence is taboo in their churches, and there is a terrible stigma attached to those who are afflicted by anything demonic. Even when they are helped, few people will stand up and testify of their newfound freedom.

Stephanie, one of our undergraduates at Biola University, had been deceived into such a bad self-concept that she developed anorexia. She was admitted to an eating-disorder clinic and underwent extensive counseling, but with little progress. One of my students suspected a spiritual problem and brought Stephanie to see me. After two counseling sessions she was free of the oppression. Stephanie returned to the clinic to tell her counselor about her free-dom in Christ. The counselor told her she was only on a temporary high. If so, Stephanie is still on it, because today she enjoys her freedom in Christ while serving the Lord on the mission field!

3. Deal with the Individual, Not the Demons

Counselees who know they are having spiritual problems usually have severe perceptual problems too. Satan seems to be more present, real, and powerful to them. These types of people usually hear opposing arguments in their head. They are constantly confronted with lies, told to get out of the counseling setting, or threatened with harm or embar-rassment.

Try to determine as much as possible about the person before any attempt at resolving the spiritual conflict. Re-member: Demons will keep a low profile until they are confronted. Once you expose them, their strategy will change to power. If you move too fast in the process, the person may try to flee in fear.

One dear lady I was counseling suddenly bolted for the door. "Tell me what you're hearing," I said.

"You're going to hurt me," she answered fearfully.

"That's a lie," I assured her. Slowly she returned to her chair.

Some people experience internal interference when demonic powers are stirred up by the truth. They may become dizzy or glassy-eyed. If you proceed without regard for their reaction they may lapse into catato-nia.

The goal in helping people find freedom in Christ is to avoid all demonic activity which would short-circuit their ability to participate in the process. With this in mind, I usually begin the steps to freedom with a prayer similar to this:

> Dear heavenly Father, I come to You in the name of the Lord Jesus Christ and by virtue of His shed blood. I acknowledge Your presence in this room and in our lives. I declare my absolute dependence on You, for apart from Christ I can do nothing. I take my position with Christ, seated with Him in the heavenlies. Because all authority in heaven and on earth has been given to Him, I now claim that authority over all enemies of the Lord Jesus Christ in and around this room and especially in (name). You have told us that where two or three are gathered in Your name You are in our midst, and that whatever is bound on earth is bound in heaven. We agree that every evil spirit that is in or around (name) be bound to silence. They cannot inflict any pain, speak to (name)'s mind, or prevent (name) from hearing, seeing, or speaking. Now in the name of the Lord Jesus Christ I command you, Satan, and all your hosts to release (name) and remain bound and gagged so that (name) will be able to obey God. In the name of Jesus I pray. Amen.

I require one major point of cooperation from all counselees: They must tell me what inner opposition they are experiencing while we are going through the steps to freedom together. If they have a thought that is contrary to what we are doing, they are to share it with me. Some thoughts can be very hostile or threatening to them. Others will be very deceptive, such as "This isn't going to work." The power of Satan is in his lie. The moment the counselees bring the contrary thought to light, the power of it is broken.

Make sure they understand that their opposing thoughts are Satan's and not their own. If they feel the thoughts are

218 • *Helping Others Find Freedom in Christ*

theirs, they will be embarrassed to share them. Assure the counselee that any thoughts which do not "joyfully concur with the law of God in the inner man" (Romans 7:22) are from Satan. They may also need to know that, given the debased nature of Satan, no thought they share with you will shock you.

I never touch the person during a counseling session, and I caution you against touching counselees also. This is hard for me because I am a hugger by nature. But until the person is free, the demonic forces in them will be repelled by the Holy Spirit in you. You typically can't get very close to a demonized person. I touched one woman on the arm to get her attention, and she later told me that she felt as though she had been violated.

I never try to restrain anyone physically, because the weapons of our warfare are not of the flesh (2 Corinthians 10:3,4). If someone runs out of my office, I let him or her go. I wait and pray, and inevitably he sheepishly pokes his head back into my office.

In difficult cases where people share the internal interference they are experiencing, I often stop and take authority again, commanding Satan to release them. I don't hide anything from the person I'm dealing with. Since every case is unique, I readily admit when I don't know what to do next. Often I will stop and pray for wisdom. I call on the individual to help me maintain control by being completely honest about the inner opposition he is experiencing. If I see him drifting away, I will ask him what he is hearing, or I will snap my fingers to get his attention. Sometimes I will stop the procedure and have him stand up and take a short walk to demonstrate that he can maintain control. I will stop the process if the opposition is too great for the counselee. In these cases, return the focus to educating him about his identity and position in Christ. He must believe the truth before he will be free.

If you ever deal with a victim of sexual or satanic ritual abuse, be prepared for major opposition. These type of people make up most of my counseling load. I really don't see how counselors who are ignorant of Satan's strongholds in the mind can have complete success with such a person. Such people often need many counseling sessions before they can walk free of bondage. Their self-concept and belief in God have been severely damaged. Many have the added neurological problem of an alternate personality which was created as a defense mechanism to help them cope with the atrocities they suffered. I used to think that Satan blocked the memories of sexual and ritual-abuse victims, but now I believe that it is *God* who blocks those memories until the person has progressed to the point of being able to process traumatic past events. Even then it is extremely difficult for these victims to overcome the effects of the past. They must come to know and accept the fact that as children of God they are not just victims of the past, but are brand-new creations in Christ, products of the work of Christ on the cross.

Deliverance is not the only step to freedom for ritual-abuse victims. Rebuilding their fractured God-concepts and self-concepts takes time, lots of love and acceptance, and the support of an understanding Christian community

4. Lead Them Through the Steps to Freedom

When it's time to lead the counselee through the steps to freedom (see Chapter 12), I prefer to have an assistant for prayer support. However, the need for an assistant is not as great in a truth encounter as in a power encounter, since no physical restraint is attempted. Out of necessity, I often deal with demonized counselees alone, and the truth still sets them free. But I always try to have a third party present when the counselee is of the opposite sex.

I give a printed copy of the prayers and doctrinal affirmations from Chapter 12 to each person present. I go through all seven steps to freedom with every counselee. I usually know which portions they need, but I don't take chances with anyone. I have them read every prayer and doctrinal affirmation aloud, explaining that Satan must hear the individual renounce him and his ways and choose to obey the Lord.

Typically, I have very little opposition when guiding a counselee to renounce non-Christian spiritual experiences. Usually little is actually resolved during this step, but the individual's renunciation of Satan and personal profession of faith in Christ is critical to the entire process.

It is common for counselees to experience significant mental opposition during the prayer and doctrinal affirmation of Step 2. They will say things like: "This isn't going to work for me"; "I want to believe it, but I just can't"; "I'm only reading this, I don't mean it." These are lies from the enemy, who is frantically trying to keep them from embracing the truth.

There was a time when I bought into that deception and thought, "Maybe this person *is* incapable of believing. Maybe it *won't* work for them." But no more. Now I respond, "Of course it's going to work"; "Of course you can believe it. If I can believe it, you can believe it. Belief is a choice"; "Of course you mean it. Every one of these statements has a scriptural base, and I know you believe the Bible."

Bitterness and unforgiveness toward other people is the most widespread stronghold that Satan enjoys among Christians. Since forgiveness must come from the heart, Step 3 is by far the most emotional step in the procedure. If it isn't, the counselee probably isn't being completely honest with himself or you.

Once the counselee has prayed the prayer in Step 3, record the names of the people that God brings to his or her mind. If he doesn't mention himself or God, I will ask him if those names need to be on his list. He usually agrees. It is not uncommon for counselees to have names come to mind which surprise them. I've had counselees remember previously repressed experiences of ritual and sexual abuse during this phase.

Stop at this point to talk about what forgiveness means and how to effect it (see Step 3 in Chapter 12). Guide the counselee through the prayer of forgiveness for each name on their list. He may hesitate to forgive some of the offenders because of the nature of the offenses suffered. But remind him that he must forgive in order to be free of the hurts of the past. The step of forgiveness is by far the most difficult, and many people are tired after completing it.

Very little opposition occurs during Steps 4 through 6. I will often read James 5:16 during the step dealing with the sins of the flesh. As the counselee talks about these issues, assure him of your acceptance and your commitment to confidentiality.

Complete freedom usually doesn't come until after the final prayer of Step 7. At that point I ask the counselee to sit comfortably and close his eyes. Then I ask, "What do you hear?" After a pause he usually responds with a relieved smile, "Nothing. It's finally quiet in my mind. I'm at peace. I'm free." I often ask those who struggled to read the doctrinal affirmation in Step 2 to read it again. They can hardly believe the ease with which they can now read and understand the scriptural statements. The countenance of many counselees often changes so markedly that I encourage them to look at themselves in a mirror. They're amazed that the joy of their freedom in Christ has even affected their appearance.

Be sure to exhort counselees that their freedom must be maintained. People who take advantage of their freedom through careless thoughts or behavior soon lose it. Satan will attempt to regain his lost ground in the days, weeks, and months ahead. But if you have instructed the counselees properly, they will know how to take a stand against him with authority. If they return to their old sinful ways they will probably end up worse than before.

SPECIAL CIRCUMSTANCES FOR SEEKING FREEDOM

I am often asked if little children can come under attack. The answer is yes. Three of my seminary students have told me about strange behavior patterns in their respective children. At times each of these kids stepped out of character and misbehaved. No attempts at discipline seemed to work. I encouraged my students to ask their children if they were having thoughts which provoked them to misbehave. In all three cases they answered yes. When these parents dealt with the deception instead of the misbehavior, the discipline problems cleared up.

One young boy who was caught lying and stealing from his parents said, "Daddy, I had to do it. Satan said he would kill you if I didn't." The boy's father later told me that if he hadn't heard me speak about the battle for the mind he would have severely disciplined his son for trying to blame the devil for his actions. Instead, he confronted the enemy's lie and hugged his son for trying to save his life. The lying and stealing stopped immediately.

A child's best defense against demonic attack is his simple, trusting faith. Children are quick to believe, and they usually understand far more than we parents give them credit for. Furthermore, your children have the added protection of being under your authority. As you carefully and prayerfully guard and nurture your freedom in Christ, chances are that your children will walk in freedom also.

I am often asked questions about demonic influences in certain locations. For example, I have received several calls from people who claim that their houses are haunted by evil spirits. Usually these conflicts are personal in nature rather than geographic, but sometimes there may be problems in a home as the result of evil activities (satanic rituals, drug dealing, etc.) which previously occurred there. Also, many Christian leaders believe in the existence of "territorial spirits" which are assigned to certain geographic locations such as countries, cities, neighborhoods, etc.

I have no absolute truth to share in these cases. If the individuals own the home they are concerned about, I encourage them to walk through the place and pray aloud, dedicating it to the Lord's use. This is the ultimate expression of good stewardship for our possessions. If they are renting or leasing the home, I suggest that they move unless the owner is a Christian and is willing to dedicate the property to the Lord.

Dear Christian, we are involved in a winnable war. Your name is written in the Lamb's book of life, and the victory has already been won. Your freedom in Christ, and the freedom of those to whom you minister, has already been secured. All you need to do is appropriate it and maintain it

I want to share one more encouraging account of victory with you. Cindy attended a Christian school and married a wonderful Christian man, but they were prevented from consummating their marriage by a series of problems. First it was an infection in Cindy's female organs. Before that could be cleared up, she began suffering horrible memories of being raped as a child by her father. She entered intense counseling but was not able to gain any real victory. Then she began remembering experiences of satanic ritual abuse in her past, and she went into an emotional tailspin.

In her desperation Cindy hopped a plane to Los Angeles and showed up on my doorstep unexpectedly. My counseling schedule was packed, but I was able to spend nearly six hours with her in one long evening session. Then she flew home. Six weeks later I received this letter:

Dear Neil:

I want to thank you again for being so gracious and available to counsel me a few weeks ago. I can truly say that God has performed a miraculous healing in me.

My entire life has been one of intense inner conflict as well as physical, emotional, and mental pain. I have lived with constant fears, recurring nightmares, continual harassment from inner voices, and an obsessive fear of death. Even though I am a committed, obedient Christian, I was convinced that Christ would certainly reject me at the gates of heaven.

A year-and-a-half ago I found that I could no longer hold the pieces of my life together. I sought counseling, and God began to provide people to minister to me and instruct me in His truth. I gained strength as I learned to claim my position in Christ as a child of God. My eyes were opened to the battle in which I was engaged.

Then last summer God allowed me to remember the horrible ritual abuse in my past, and the battle became much more intense. I had to spend hours every day and night in God's Word, in prayer and meditation, and in direct confrontation and resistance of the enemy. After two months of very little sleep and virtually no peace or rest, I was certain that only Christ could deliver me from my internal hell.

Prior to leaving for Los Angeles to see you, God encouraged me with several passages of Scripture: Psalm 11:7; Micah 7:7,8; Job 23:10. Our counseling session was a vital tool that God used in my healing process. After several hours of reliving the horrors of my past and forgiving the 22 people who had sexually abused me, I was finally free from Satan's bondage. Praise God that He went before me and defeated Satan at the cross (Hebrews 2:14,15).

Neil, I'm so happy that I am free and that I have a sound mind! I no longer have to hide the hell inside with a happy Christian facade. God gave me Isaiah 51:3 as a picture of what He has done in me: "Indeed, the Lord will comfort...all her waste places. And her wilderness He will make like Eden, and her desert like the garden of the Lord; joy and gladness will be found in her, thanksgiving and sound of a melody."

With love,

Cindy

Have you met the Bondage Breaker? Jesus Christ will set you free!

For information concerning training and resource material write to:

Freedom In Christ Ministries
491 East Lambert Road
La Habra, CA 90631

APPENDICES

===

Further Help!

The Christian's Scriptural Identity and Position

The following statements summarize your scriptural identity and position in Christ and form the foundation for your freedom in Christ. Read these statements aloud often. If you are presently involved in a spiritual conflict, read these statements aloud at least once each day for a month.

Who Am I?

Exodus

I am *not* the great "I am" (3:14; John 8:24,28,58), but by the grace of God, I am what I am (1 Corinthians 15:10).

Matthew

I am the salt of the earth (5:13).

I am the light of the world (5:14).

John

I am a child of God (1:12).

I am part of the true vine, a channel of Christ's life (15:1,5).

I am Christ's friend (15:15).

I am chosen and appointed by Christ to bear His fruit (15:16).

Romans

I am a slave of righteousness (6:18).

I am enslaved to God (6:22).

I am a son of God; God is spiritually my Father (8:14,15; Galatians 3:26; 4:6).

I am a joint heir with Christ, sharing His inheritance with Him (8:17).

1 Corinthians

I am a temple—a dwelling place—of God. His Spirit and His life dwell in me (3:16; 6:19).

I am united to the Lord and am one spirit with Him (6:17).

I am a member of Christ's body (12:27; Ephesians 5:30).

2 Corinthians

I am a new creation (5:17).

I am reconciled to God and am a minister of reconciliation (5:18,19).

Galatians

I am a son of God and one in Christ (3:26,28).

I am an heir of God since I am a son of God (4:6,7).

Ephesians

I am a saint (1:1; 1 Corinthians 1:2; Philippians 1:1; Colossians 1:2).

I am God's workmanship—His handiwork—born anew in Christ to do His work (2:10).

I am a fellow citizen with the rest of God's family (2:19).

I am a prisoner of Christ (3:1; 4:1).

I am righteous and holy (4:24).

Philippians

I am a citizen of heaven, seated in heaven right now (3:20; Ephesians 2:6).

Colossians

I am hidden with Christ in God (3:3).

I am an expression of the life of Christ because He is my life (3:4).

I am chosen of God, holy and dearly loved (3:12; 1 Thessalonians 1:4).

1 Thessalonians

I am a son of light and not of darkness (5:5).

Hebrews

I am a holy partaker of a heavenly calling (3:1).

I am a partaker of Christ; I share in His life (3:14).

1 Peter

I am one of God's living stones, being built up in Christ as a spiritual house (2:5).

I am a member of a chosen race, a royal priesthood, a holy nation, a people for God's own possession (2:9,10).

I am an alien and stranger to this world in which I temporarily live (2:11).

I am an enemy of the devil (5:8).

1 John

I am a child of God and I will resemble Christ when He returns (3:1,2).

I am born of God, and the evil one—the devil—cannot touch me (5:18).

The above has been taken from Neil T. Anderson, *Victory Over the Darkness* (Regal Books, 1990). Used by permission.

SINCE I AM IN CHRIST, BY THE GRACE OF GOD...

Romans

I have been justified—completely forgiven and made righteous (5:1).

I died with Christ and died to the power of sin's rule over my life (6:1-6).

I am free forever from condemnation (8:1).

1 Corinthians

I have been placed into Christ by God's doing (1:30).

I have received the Spirit of God into my life that I might know the things freely given to me by God (2:12).

I have been given the mind of Christ (2:16).

I have been bought with a price; I am not my own; I belong to God (6:19,20).

2 Corinthians

I have been established, anointed, and sealed by God in Christ, and I have been given the Holy Spirit as a pledge guaranteeing my inheritance to come (1:21; Ephesians 1:13,14).

Since I have died, I no longer live for myself, but for Christ (5:14,15).

I have been made righteous (5:21).

Galatians

I have been crucified with Christ, and it is no longer I who live, but Christ lives in me. The life I am now living is Christ's life (2:20).

Ephesians

I have been blessed with every spiritual blessing (1:3).

I was chosen in Christ before the foundation of the world to be holy, and I am without blame before Him (1:4).

I was predestined—determined by God—to be adopted as God's son (1:5).

I have been redeemed and forgiven, and I am a recipient of His lavish grace (1:6-8).

I have been made alive together with Christ (2:5).

I have been raised up and seated with Christ in heaven (2:6).

I have direct access to God through the Spirit (2:18).

I may approach God with boldness, freedom, and confidence (3:12).

Colossians

I have been rescued from the domain of Satan's rule and transferred to the kingdom of Christ (1:13).

I have been redeemed and forgiven of all my sins. The debt against me has been canceled (1:14).

Christ Himself is in me (1:27).

I am firmly rooted in Christ and am now being built up in Him (2:7).

I have been made complete in Christ (2:10).

I have been buried, raised, and made alive with Christ (2:12,13).

I died with Christ and I have been raised up with Christ. My life is now hidden with Christ in God. Christ is now my life (3:1-4).

2 Timothy

I have been given a Spirit of power, love, and self-discipline (1:7).

I have been saved and set apart according to God's doing (1:9; Titus 3:5).

Hebrews

Because I am sanctified and am one with the Sanctifier, He is not ashamed to call me His brother (2:11).

I have the right to come boldly before the throne of God to receive mercy and find grace to help in time of need (4:16).

2 Peter

I have been given precious and magnificent promises by God, by which I am a partaker of God's divine nature (1:4).

Non-Christian Spiritual Experience Inventory

Circle any of the following activities in which you have been involved in any way.

Occult
astral projection
Ouija board
table lifting
speaking in a trance
automatic writing
visionary dreams
telepathy
ghosts
materialization
clairvoyance
clairsentience
fortune-telling
tarot cards
palm-reading
astrology
rod and pendulum
  (dowsing)
amateur hypnosis
healing magnetism
magic charming
mental suggestion
black and white
  magic
blood pacts
fetishism
incubi and succubi
  (sexual spirits)

Cult
Christian Science
Unity
Scientology
The Way Interna-
  tional
Unification Church
Church of the
  Living Word
Mormonism
Jehovah's Witnesses
Children of God
Swedenborgianism
H.W. Armstrong
  (Worldwide
  Church of God)
Unitarianism
Masons
New Age
Other ____

Other Religions
Zen Buddhism
Hare Krishna
Bahaism
Rosicrucianism
Science of Mind
Science of Crea-
  tive Intelligence
Hinduism
Transcendental
  Meditation
Yoga
Eckankar
Roy Masters
Silva Mind Control
Father Divine
Theosophical
  Society
Islam
Black Muslim
Other ____

1. Have you ever been hypnotized, attended a New Age seminar, or participated in a seance?

2. Have you ever taken a class or read books on para-psychology? Explain.

3. Have you ever heard voices in your mind or had repeating and nagging thoughts that were foreign to what you believe or feel, like there was a dialogue going on in your head? Explain.

4. What other spiritual experiences have you had that would be considered out of the ordinary?

Confidential Personal Inventory

I. Personal Information

Name _____ Telephone (___) _____

Address _____

Church affiliation

  Present _____

  Past _____

School

  Highest grade completed ___ Degrees earned _____

Marital status _____

Previous marriage/divorce _____

Vocation

  Present _____

  Past _____

II. Family History

  A. Religious

    1. To your knowledge, have any of your parents, grandparents, or great-grandparents ever been involved in any occultic, cultic, or non-Christian religious practices? Please refer to the Non-Christian Spiritual Experience Inventory and indicate what their involvement was.

2. Briefly explain your parents' Christian experience (i.e., were they Christians, and did they profess and live their Christianity?).

B. Marital Status

1. Are your parents presently married or divorced? Explain.

2. Was there a sense of security and harmony in your home during the first 12 years of your life?

3. Was your father clearly the head of the home, or was there a role reversal in which your mother ruled the home? Explain.

4. How did your father treat your mother?

5. To your knowledge, were any of your parents or grandparents ever involved in an adulterous affair?

C Health
   1. Are there any addictive problems in your family (alcohol, drugs, etc.)?

   2. Is there any history of mental illness?

   3. Is there any history of the following ailments in your family (please circle)?

      tuberculosis (TB)   heart disease
      diabetes   cancer
      ulcers   glandular problems
      other

   4. How would you describe your family's concern for:
      a) diet
      b) exercise
      c) rest

D. Moral Climate

During the first 18 years of your life, how would you rate the moral atmosphere in which you were raised?

	Overly Permissive	Permissive	Average	Strict	Overly Strict
clothing	5	4	3	2	1
sex	5	4	3	2	1
dating	5	4	3	2	1
movies	5	4	3	2	1
music	5	4	3	2	1
literature	5	4	3	2	1
free will	5	4	3	2	1
drinking	5	4	3	2	1
smoking	5	4	3	2	1
church attendance	5	4	3	2	1

III. History of Personal Health
A. Physical

1. Describe your eating habits (i.e., junk food addict, eat regularly or sporadically, balanced diet, etc.).

2. Do you have any addictions or cravings that you find difficult to control (sweets, drugs, alcohol, food in general, etc.)?

3. Are you presently under any kind of medication for either physical or psychological reasons?

4. Do you have any problem sleeping? Are you having recurring nightmares or disturbances?

5. Does your present schedule allow for regular periods of rest and relaxation?

6. Are you adopted?

7. Have you ever been physically beaten or sexually molested? Explain.

B. Mental
   1. Which of the following have you struggled with

in the past or are you struggling with presently (please check)?

—— daydreaming
—— lustful thoughts
—— thoughts of inferiority
—— thoughts of inadequacy
—— worry
—— doubts
—— fantasy
—— obsessive thoughts
—— insecurity
—— blasphemous thoughts
—— compulsive thoughts
—— dizziness
—— headaches

2. Do you spend much time wishing you were somebody else or fantasizing that you were a different person? Do you imagine yourself living at a different time, in a different place, or under different circumstances? Explain.

3. How many hours of TV to you watch per week? —————— List your five favorite programs.

4. How many hours do you spend each week reading? _____ What do you read primarily (newspaper, magazines, books, etc.)?

5. Would you consider yourself to be an optimist or a pessimist (i.e., do you have a tendency to see the good in people and life or the bad?)?

6. Have you ever thought that maybe you were "cracking up"? Do you presently fear that possibility? Explain.

7. Do you have regular devotions in the Bible? Where and when, and to what extent?

8. Do you find prayer difficult mentally? Explain.

9. When attending church or other Christian ministries, are you plagued by foul thoughts, jealousies, or other mental harassment? Explain.

10. Do you listen to music a lot? What type do you enjoy most?

C Emotional
1. Which of the following emotions have you had difficulty controlling or are you presently having difficulty controlling (please circle)?

___ frustration	___ fear of death
___ anger	___ fear of losing your
___ anxiety	mind
___ loneliness	___ fear of committing
___ worthlessness	suicide
___ depression	___ fear of hurting
___ hatred	loved ones
___ bitterness	___ fear of _____

2. Which of the above listed emotions do you feel are sinful? Why?

3. Concerning your emotions, whether positive or negative, which of the following best describes you (please check)?

____ readily express them

____ express some of my emotions, but not all

____ readily acknowledge their presence, but am reserved in expressing them

____ tendency to suppress my emotions

____ find it safest not to express how I feel

____ tendency to disregard how I feel since I cannot trust my feelings

____ consciously or subconsciously deny them; it's too painful to deal with them

4. Do you presently know someone with whom you could be emotionally honest (i.e., you could tell this person exactly how you feel about yourself, life, and other people)?

5. How important is it that we are emotionally honest before God? Do you feel that you are? Explain.

IV. Spiritual History

A. If you were to die tonight, do you know where you would spend eternity?

B. Suppose you die tonight and appear before God in heaven, and He asks you, "By what right should I allow you into My presence?" How would you answer Him?

C. First John 5:11,12 says, "God has given us eternal life, and this life is in His Son. He who has the Son has the life; he who does not have the Son of God does not have the life."

1. Do you have the Son of God in you?

2. When did you receive Him (John 1:12)?

3. How do you know that you received Him?

D. Are you plagued by doubts about your salvation?

E. Are you presently enjoying fellowship with other believers, and if so, where and when?

F. Are you under the authority of a local church where the Bible is taught? Do you regularly support it with your time, talent, and treasure? If not, why not?

G. Please fill out the Non-Christian Spiritual Experience Inventory.

NOTES

Chapter 1—You Don't Have to Live in the Shadows
1. Conversation with Dr. Paul Hiebert, who teaches in the School of Missions at Fuller Theological Seminary, Pasadena, CA.

Chapter 2—Finding Your Way in the World
1. C. Fred Dickason, *Demon Possession and the Christian* (Chicago: Moody Press, 1987), p. 226-27.

Chapter 5—Jesus Has You Covered
1. Jessie Penn-Lewis, *War on the Saints*, 9th ed. (New York: Thomas E. Lowe, Ltd., 1973).
2. Theodore H. Epp *Praying with Authority* (Lincoln, NE: Back to the Bible Broadcast, 1965), p. 98.
3. Dickason, *Demon Possession and the Christian*, p. 255.

Chapter 6—Dealing with Evil in Person
1. C.S. Lewis, *The Screwtape Letters* (Old Tappan, NJ: Fleming H. Revell, 1978).
2. Michael Scanlan, T.O.R., and Randall J. Cirner, *Deliverance from Evil Spirits* (Ann Arbor, MI: Servant Books, 1980), p. 16.
3. Everett Ferguson, *Demonology of the Early Christian World*, Symposium Series, Vol. 12 (New York: Edwin Mellen Press, 1984), p. 118.

Chapter 10—Appearances Can Be Deceiving
1. Quoted from Martin Wells Knapp, *Impressions* (Wheaton, IL: Tyndale House Publishing, Inc., 1984), p. 14-15.

Chapter 11—The Danger of Losing Control
1. Merrill F. Unger, *What Demons Can Do to Saints* (Chicago: Moody Press, 1977), p. 51.
2. Ibid.
3. Ibid.

Chapter 12—Steps to Freedom in Christ
1. Ferguson, *Demonology*, p. 130.
2. Ibid., p. 127.

Victory Over the Darkness

by Neil T. Anderson

Realising the power of your identity in Christ.

'Being in Christ, and all that it means to Christian identity and freedom, is the overwhelming theme of the New Testament...if you see yourself as a child of God who is spiritually alive in Christ, you'll begin to live in victory and freedom.'

Every day millions of Christians live below par—emotionally, physically, spiritually. Because they do not grasp the central fact of their identity in Christ, they miss out on the freedom and maturity they should enjoy. This life-transforming book is for everyone who longs for spiritual growth.

'I cannot recommend this book highly enough... *Victory Over the Darkness* points the way to true liberty and victory in Jesus.'—Colin Urquhart.

ISBN 1 85424 183 4   256pp, £4.99

Monarch Publications

Living Free in Christ

by Neil T. Anderson

'We are no longer products of our past. We are products of Christ's work on the cross.'

When we become Christians, we are given new identities as children of God. We are forgiven. Each of us becomes a saint, a child of light, a divine masterpiece, a citizen of heaven.

But we still conform to the patterns of our previous lives. We don't receive the full measure of what God has in store for us as Christians. There is no automatic 'delete' button on past programming. 'If we do not see ourselves as God sees us,' comments Neil Anderson, 'then we suffer from a wrong identity and a poor image of who we really are'.

To help us to realise our true identity in full, Dr Anderson discusses in detail more than thirty verses relating to our acceptance, security and significance in Christ—'our most critical and foundational needs'. Each chapter is illustrated with a variety of examples from Dr Anderson's extensive pastoral ministry, and concludes with a prayer to help us respond more deeply.

ISBN 1 85424 217 2   288pp, £4.99

Monarch Publications

Monarch Publications

Books of Substance

All Monarch books can be purchased from your local
Christian or general bookshop. In case of difficulty they may
be ordered from the publisher:

> Monarch Publications
> Broadway House
> The Broadway
> Crowborough
> East Sussex
> TN6 1HQ

Please enclose a cheque payable to Monarch Publications for
the cover price plus: 60p for the first book ordered plus 40p
per copy for each additional book, to a maximum charge of
£3.00 to cover postage and packing (UK and Republic of
Ireland only).

Overseas customers please order from:

> Christian Marketing PTY Ltd
> PO Box 519
> Belmont
> Victoria 3216
> Australia

> Omega Distributors Ltd
> 69 Great South Road
> Remuera
> Auckland
> New Zealand

> Struik Christian Books
> 80 McKenzie Street Gardens
> Cape Town 8001
> South Africa